On Learning
GOLF

BY

PERCY BOOMER

FOREWORD BY THE DUKE OF WINDSOR

ALFRED · A · KNOPF · NEW YORK
1946

THIS IS A BORZOI BOOK
PUBLISHED BY ALFRED A. KNOPF, INC.

Copyright 1946 by Percy Boomer. All rights reserved. No part of this book may be reproduced in any form without permission in writing from the publisher, except by a reviewer who may quote brief passages or reproduce not more than three illustrations in a review to be printed in a magazine or newspaper.

Manufactured in the United States of America.

FIRST AMERICAN EDITION

A "GOOD OUT"

PERCY

FOREWORD

By The Duke of Windsor

IN the years before the war when there was more leisure to play and study golf, I tried to help Percy Boomer evolve some of the ideas which he presents in his book. This may be the reason why he has asked me from among all his more proficient pupils to write a foreword, and because he used to find me the most persistent in the search for the secret of the correct swing.

Golf has been the subject of so much writing that Percy Boomer is to be congratulated on developing some original thoughts on the popular pastime. Although no game has produced more theories or evoked a greater divergence of opinion as to the methods of its teaching, I believe even the author's sternest critics will admit that he has achieved a pleasing combination of humour with plenty of good golf sense.

It is in no way Percy Boomer's fault that I have not yet discovered the elusive secret, and it has to be as a disciple of the game and not as a low-handicap player that I recommend *On Learning Golf,* in the hope that it will help to reduce its readers' scores and discourage their opponents.

CONTENTS

Plan of the Course   xi

PART ONE

The Genesis of This Book   3

CHAPTER I. *What Teaching Taught Me*   11
CHAPTER II. *Fundamentals (1) Golf and the Senses*   16
CHAPTER III. *Fundamentals (2) The Swing*   23
CHAPTER IV. *Golf Bogey No. 1*   29
CHAPTER V. *The Road to Golfing Health*   35
CHAPTER VI. *The Concentration Fallacy*   40

PART TWO

On Learning and Teaching   49

CHAPTER VII. *The Controlled Golf Swing*   56
CHAPTER VIII. *Preparatory to the Swing*   68
CHAPTER IX. *Interlude for Instruction—What we Mean When we Say*   79
CHAPTER X. *Centered on Wrist Action*   89

Contents

CHAPTER	XI.	To Keep—or Not to Keep—Your Eye on the Ball	101
CHAPTER	XII.	Interlude for Instruction—It is the Pupil Who Must Learn	113
CHAPTER	XIII.	The Feeling of "In-to-Out"	124
CHAPTER	XIV.	The Force Center	133
CHAPTER	XV.	Interlude for Instruction—Monologue	146
CHAPTER	XVI.	Rhythm	155
CHAPTER	XVII.	Interlude for Instruction—As a Dancer Sees It	169
CHAPTER	XVIII.	Power	177
CHAPTER	XIX.	Interlude for Instruction—A Mathematician Explains	187
CHAPTER	XX.	Temperament	196
CHAPTER	XXI.	Interlude for Instruction—Largely Concerned with the Waggle	208
CHAPTER	XXII.	Putting	220
CHAPTER	XXIII.	Interlude for Reminiscence	233
CHAPTER	XXIV.	Golf Analysis	240
CHAPTER	XXV.	Inverse Functioning	249

ILLUSTRATIONS

A "Good Out"	FRONTISPIECE
Nearing the Top of the Swing	faces page 28
The Address	74
The Grip	100
Correct "Feel" of the Swing	128
Nearing the Finish	154
The Golf Swing in Embryo	168
Reversed or Putting Grip	224
The Swing	246

PLAN OF THE COURSE

o

THIS is not a book on the science of golf, but about learning it. Everything on the science of the game has been written, little on how to learn it. So I outline a method of learning and stress certain points about the golf swing. And please remember that long experience has told me what to emphasize when teaching. Some of the points which you will find me making a fuss about are considered minor details in the science of the game, but they are important to me because they relate to feel rather than to mechanics—and it is through *feel* that I play and teach.

I believe that the mechanical details, like the ball, should become incidental. They are of course of extraordinary interest and if this book arouses interest in the fundamental sensations of the golf swing I shall be tempted to write another (and much more extensive one) on its detail. But that is another matter.

In brief, the plan of this book is that in the six chapters of Part One I outline my *theory* of golf, and explain how I came by it and why I hold it; while Part Two consists of chapters which elaborate the various technical points, interspersed with Interludes for Instruction and Reminiscence which enable certain very essential points to be emphasized as well as providing a little light relief from the more solid matter.

Plan of the Course

Finally, this book could not possibly be complete without the magnificent photographs which my friends Val Doone have been at such generous pains to make for me. In the course of my golfing life (a grand one!) I have seen thousands of golfing photographs, and they were mostly all just the usual and rather useless pictures; they did not, as do these, reproduce most faithfully those subtleties of grip and stance, of the play of essential muscles, and of the poise of limb and club in motion—which are, in the end, the grail we seek.

PERCY BOOMER

ON LEARNING GOLF

Part One

THE GENESIS OF THIS BOOK

o

GOLF is in the Boomer blood. My father was a village schoolmaster in Jersey. As an educationist he was generations ahead of his time. He saw no use in forcing a boy to try to learn subjects which he was obviously incapable of absorbing—and of which he could make no use anyway, but he did help his pupils to develop such talents and natural aptitudes as they possessed.

In consequence, though so far as I know his school never produced a Senior Wrangler and maybe did not show up too well when the Inspector came round, it did have the very remarkable record of producing five golfers of international rank in one generation.

I imagine that it is a world's record for a village school and one never likely to be beaten and if any memorial were needed to my father's devotion to the game the records of the great Channel Island golfers who were his pupils—incomparable Harry Vardon and his brothers Tom and Alfred, the three Gaudins, Renouf, and Ted Ray—would provide it.

Harry Vardon wrote as follows in the story of his golfing life:

> In due course we all went to the village school but I fear, from all that I can remember, and from what I have been told that knowledge had little attraction for me in those days, and I know I often played truant sometimes three weeks at a stretch. Consequently my old school-

On Learning Golf

master Mr. Boomer had no particular reason to be proud of me at that time, as he seems to have become since.

He never enjoys a holiday so much in these days as when he comes over from Jersey to see me play for the Open Championship, as he does whenever the meeting is held at Sandwich. But when I did win the championship on that course he was so nervous and excited about my prospects that he felt himself unequal to watching me and during most of the time I was doing my four rounds he was sitting in a fretful state on the seashore.

Incidentally when my father retired from schoolteaching at the age of sixty, he joined me at St. Cloud and became a professional golfer. My brother Aubrey became a Pro at seventeen, and now my son George —having had his schooling cut short by the European upheavals—has started his chosen career at sixteen.

About myself. It was intended that I should follow my father as a schoolmaster, but as it fell out I preceded him as a golf Pro! After very few years of schoolteaching I decided that any talents I had lay elsewhere and being by then a pretty good amateur golfer I obtained the job of 8th Assistant at Queen's Park, Bournemouth. I was then twenty-two. After a short period at Bournemouth I moved to Barton-on-Sea, and from Barton to St. Cloud in 1913. My long period at St. Cloud was interrupted by the first Great War (when I served in the Royal Naval Air Service) and at least broken again by the second. It was at St. Cloud that I developed my ideas about the game and built up my experience as a teacher of it.

The Genesis of This Book

Though I have never had the physique required for the hard mill of championship golf I have won three International Open Championships, the Belgian in 1923, the Swiss in 1924, and the Dutch in 1927.

My brother Aubrey is thirteen years my junior. He joined me at St. Cloud when he was seventeen, with a fine athletic record at Victoria College behind him. Shortly after he also joined the R.N.A.S. and we both returned to St. Cloud early in 1919. In our first fourball match together there we played the two top Americans in the Inter-Allied games. The Yanks won the tournament, but Aubrey and I halved our match.

The best Aubrey has done in the British Open was second to Bobby Jones at St. Andrews. He holds the record for the French Open having won it five times; he has also won the Belgian and Dutch titles several times and the Italian once. By winning the *Daily Mail* tournament, the *Glasgow Evening Herald* meeting at Gleneagles and the Roehampton show, he played himself into the British team in three matches against the Americans—two of them for the Ryder Cup.

It is also not to be forgotten that Aubrey holds the world's record for a single round. His 61 was done at St. Cloud in a French P.G.A. tournament against the American Ryder Cup team. The tournament was won by Horton Smith, Aubrey following him in second place.

Aubrey holds many course records, but I suppose the most curious one is that he has never played a shot

On Learning Golf

over the course on which Harry Vardon learned his golf—though he was born in the parish in which the course lies, and indeed no more than a mile from the house in which the Vardons were born.

That was at Grouville, on the east of the island, and before Aubrey reached golfing age our family had moved to the other end of the island, where—characteristically enough—my father proceeded to build the Le Moye course with the help of his family and a few friends. Cutting greens out of that magnificent natural golf terrain was my first introduction to golf architecture.

Aubrey and I toured the Argentine together. We were in fact the first visiting Pros to do so—and the first to play that dynamic golfer José Jurado. I have always considered that the tournament that Aubrey won there against the best of their Pros and in most difficult and unfamiliar conditions, one of his finest feats.

Some years ago I was playing in a four-ball match with George (Theory) Duncan, my brother Aubrey, and Mr. E. Esmond. We were discussing a shot that Aubrey had just played and Mr. Esmond said to George, "You know Percy was a schoolmaster at one time." George looked at me with his quaint grin and said, "I thought so—he plays like one!"

He was quite right, though it is not because of my early school-teaching that my game looks as studied and considered as it does. The truth is that though I

The Genesis of This Book

learned the game in Jersey as soon as I could walk and Harry Vardon was my boyhood idol, I was not what is known as a natural golfer. There is nothing instinctive about my game. Everything I have ever done in golf I had to *learn to do*. Maybe having to teach myself was not a bad preparation for my future work of teaching others.

As a boy I was just a plodder, but I stuck to it and before I took my first professional job I was a good three handicap amateur and held the amateur record of Le Moye with 78. I went back there a few years ago and did an approximate 64 in a four-ball match—nearly a stroke a hole better as a result of twenty-five years' hard work and study. But probably the more valuable gain was in the matter of *consistency* and in being able to play my best when I *needed* to play my best.

Do not think that this consistency and control "come naturally" to a professional. Far from it. My first shot as a Pro was at Meyrick Park, Bournemouth—and I topped it! Indeed the whole time I was with the Bournemouth Club I hardly hit a single really clean shot from that tee. *The very fact that my living depended upon my golf made a shot which as an amateur I should have found easy enough, one of almost insuperable difficulty.* Keep that in mind please, and so remember that when I talk of golfing "nerves" I have had practical experience.

It was probably due to my father's influence that when I set out seriously to teach myself golf, I decided

On Learning Golf

I must teach myself a *simple* style. For my father was always insisting that *simplicity* was the greatest of all gifts and the most laudable of all attainments. To illustrate this, he took me to London to see Gerald du Maurier act. How utterly easy he made acting look! You were not conscious of the years of toil that must have gone to the building of that superb technique. Remember that when next you envy the effortless ease with which a crack Pro drives!

So it came about that I set out at first to find a simple swing and then, at a later date to find a simple method of imparting this to others. The discovery, or rather the development of the swing itself was not so difficult, but it is only comparatively recently that I have learned how to teach it. And I freely admit that the teaching is still less simple than I would like it to be.

I have started to write this book twenty times in the last twenty years and I might still hesitate to write it had I nothing more than the theory of a satisfactory swing to impart. But now, teed up for my twenty-first start, I know I am going on until the book is finished. And why? Because this time I feel I have a solid contribution to offer to the teaching and learning of golf. It is upon an aspect of the matter which has been practically ignored by writers, teachers and players alike—but one which I have proved beyond doubt to be of fundamental importance.

So in this book, superimposed upon the fruits of my knowledge, experience, and theories of the game, you

The Genesis of This Book

will find my account of the relation between the physical and the psychological in golf—a relationship which lies at the root of every form of *control*—of both individual shots and of one's game as a whole. Until I realized the importance of this relationship and discovered how to use it everything that I wrote seemed *inconclusive*. At so many points there seemed nothing further to be done but to shrug one's shoulders and repeat "Golf is a funny game!" But once the relationship between mental and physical was rightly realized these blanks filled in—and the practical results in teaching were astounding.

CHAPTER I

What Teaching Taught Me

o

ANYONE who has taught golf or who has even watched closely a number of beginners at the game knows that there are two great classes—those who are *natural* golfers and those who are not. My brother Aubrey was born a golfer; I had to make myself one and a hard time I had doing it. Indeed we were both extreme members of our respective classes.

A study of the difference in mental and physical make-up between the *natural* golfer and the *made* one is intensely interesting. So is a study of their ultimate capacity for the game. Not all the advantages are on the side of the natural player. Of course if his early game is guided by a far-seeing nature, as Aubrey's was, he is fortunate. But too often the natural golfer is so successful at first that he is content to be self-taught—and the self-taught golfer is usually a *badly* taught one. Why? Well for a number of reasons which this book will make clear, not the least important being the fact that the soundest and most permanently profitable motions in golf feel unnatural and "all wrong" to most people when first tried.

Further we are all imitative to some degree and unless we learn a whole and comprehensive technique

On Learning Golf

of the game from a teacher who has a coherent idea of the relationship of the various shots, we are apt to pick up a bit here and a bit there by watching others. The result is a patchwork game, full of pretty shots maybe when it is running well, but so loosely hung together and so self-contradictory in some of its component parts that it is *unreliable* and may be expected to break down or blow up when the strain comes.

A well-taught golfer rarely breaks down and rarely goes off his game completely and if he does strike a bad patch one or at the most two lessons will pull him back again. But patching up a badly taught player is one of the most difficult and thankless tasks a teacher can undertake. I have refused to take on hundreds of such cases, because I do not believe that any instruction that is not part of a *consistent* system can be of any permanent benefit.

"Tips" which are guaranteed to improve your game are easy enough to come by. Every club-house is full of them, and you have only to go a few holes with a friend to know what his own particular disease is by the "cures" he hands out to you! It is human nature to feel sure that everyone else is afflicted by the same troubles as those which torment ourselves. But all this advice is dangerous for it is just *impossible* to build up a sound game by accepting tips and instructions and advice from all those who are willing to offer them.

Does this apply only if we copy or take advice from

What Teaching Taught Me

bad examples? Oh no!—anyone from a beginner to an experienced golfer who has tried to take too much expert advice from too many sources will have been baffled and confused both in his mind and in his style by the opposite theories and contradictory practices of acknowledged masters. This fact alone is sufficient to prove one of the main contentions of this book, that the mechanical muscular movements employed in golf are not the whole secret of it.

The truth about the conflicting theories of experts is quite simple. The masters play as it suits them to play and then evolve theories to explain why the particular movements which they discover themselves employing are *right*! Unfortunately a shot that may be effective enough in the hands of a master may have disastrous results if "copied" by some less expert player.

Of course the muscular-mechanical movements in golf are extremely important but they are not everything. After teaching myself first and then for thirty-five years teaching others, I have arrived at concrete conclusions as to what the important factors are and I would summarize them roughly as follows:

1. Every good golf shot is the outcome of a satisfactory psychological-physical relationship.
2. It is this relationship which gives *control* and *consistency*.
3. These good relationships (and consequent controls) are built up most easily and firmly when the

On Learning Golf

muscular-mechanical requirements of the game have been simplified.

And so—

  4. It is desirable to learn to play as many of the shots as possible *with the same movements.*

Let me illustrate this last point which is fundamental in my theory of teaching, by describing the case of a pupil of mine, a lady no longer young who came to me more or less in despair. She had tried hard to play golf but had been defeated because she had never succeeded in driving even one hundred yards!

I taught her golf *with one club only,* her driver, and only off the tee. All I taught her was *how to drive.* When she came to me later and said, "How do I play pitch shots?" I replied, "As you drive." When she asked, "How do I putt?" I replied again, "As you drive."

I continued, "As the shot, and consequently the club, becomes shorter, we stand a little more open to the hole and draw the feet closer together and bring the ball back nearer to the right foot. When playing with the driver the ball will be placed just inside the line of the left heel—with a No. 8 iron it will be just inside the right heel."

I did not need to explain to her that the more we face the hole the nearer to the line of flight will the club head go back—or that the nearer we stand to the ball the more vertical will be our swing (because we

What Teaching Taught Me

are looking more directly down, our shoulders *dip* more on the way back and in consequence our club head comes up more steeply "naturally"). I did not need to explain these points because the correct action is the natural outcome of the position taken up—provided that the fundamentals of the swing are not interfered with.

Teaching golf as *all one shot* simplified her game. It prevented her other shots from interfering with her drive or her drive confusing her other shots, because all the shots were fundamentally the same. And though this pupil was taught with a driver only she now plays the most delicate run-up shots, and pitches excellently, in fact, she runs up better than do many players with handicaps lower than her own 15. Incidentally I look on that 15 as one of the outstanding proofs of the soundness of the theories propounded in this book.

The fault with much of the golf teaching of today, professional as well as amateur, is that the teacher tries to eradicate specific faults by issuing specific instructions. In short, the "good tip" system again. This is fatal, mainly because it is no system at all but just a conglomeration of golf patent medicines. The true aim of the teacher who desires to build up a sound and dependable game in a pupil, must be to link up in the pupil a *line of controls*. And for reasons which will become obvious as this book is read, the aim of the pupil must be to carry out the teacher's instructions *irrespective of immediate results.*

CHAPTER II

Fundamentals

1. GOLF AND THE SENSES

EVERY intelligent person who has played golf must have speculated on the relation between the mental and the physical aspects of the game. This is one of the fundamental problems of golf and I had early reason to think about it, for as already related—as soon as I had become a professional the very fact that I *had* become a Pro seemed to have made it impossible for me to hit a decent shot from the first tee at Meyrick Park. Why? If we could find the answer to that we should understand golf "nerves" and maybe see how to avoid them.

When we consider the make-up of a good games player we usually start with a catalogue of *physical* qualities, such as a good eye, steely wrists, good reach, etc. To these we may add—if we are advanced enough to be conscious of psychology—two or three purely mental qualities, such as "good nerves" and intelligence. For years and years I tried to strike a fair balance between the qualities in the two groups, and decided at various times that golf was 50 per cent physical and 50 per cent mental, then 40 per cent/60 per cent and 80 per cent/20 per cent, and all sorts of other proportions. But I admit that however I considered the matter I never felt convinced that I had

Golf and the Senses

found a correct answer. I already knew that we played reflex golf, and that a reflex was muscular memory, and this should have told me that any clear-cut division between mental and physical was impossible. I now know why!

Of course this division of golf into separate physical and mental departments was not an idea of my own. It was the way we all thought about the game. I remember spending one of the most stimulating evenings of my life listening to—and occasionally chipping in on—a debate on the light-ball, between some Americans and members of the Committee of the R. & A. Walter Hagen was there and members of the Ryder Cup team. For myself, though I enjoyed the argument immensely, I felt even at that time that it was *inconclusive;* something was lacking again. I think I had got so far as to realize that the arguments advanced lacked conclusiveness *because they were either too purely mental or too purely physical.*

I had in fact reached the conclusion that any separation of the mental and physical functions in the playing or teaching of golf must be artificial—because in the practical job of playing or teaching no such separation is possible.

But though I had reached this conclusion and was increasingly basing my teaching on it, I found it most difficult to express the idea explicitly—even to myself. Then by one of those happy chances which do occur when you are ripe for them, I read a remarkable little

On Learning Golf

book, *The Use of the Self* by F. Matthias Alexander.

It was the confirmation and exposition I had wanted. For here was a man with profound knowledge of psychology and physiology surveying the whole field of human activity and expressing scientifically the very truth which I had sensed, but found so difficult to express, in the sphere of golf.

Professor Alexander's conclusion is that we never act purely psychologically or purely physically, but that every act is carried out in psychophysical unison. And further, that when this unison is functioning properly it provides a form of *conscious control* which is precisely what a golfer needs.

I realized at once that this *conscious control* was exactly what I was already trying to teach because I recognized it as a form of control *that would replace thinking*. And thinking had to be replaced because I knew by experience that if your golf was dependent upon *thinking* it was at the mercy of your mental state. Excitement, depression, elation—any emotion could destroy you.

I had always been considered a good teacher, but I had never been satisfied because I could not teach a pupil to play exactly and consistently—independent of his mental and physical feelings and of the state of the game. And I felt that I ought to be able to teach this. And now I am able to do so, provided that the pupil is willing to work at the game on a "long term" policy.

Golf and the Senses

With my broadening view of the relation between physical and mental, and the possibilities of conscious control I have definitely gained a new capacity in teaching, enabling me to build up in my pupils one control upon another, by building up *feel*. I build up a *feel* of what is right in his golf. So when he gets to the first tee in front of a gallery or is faced by a tricky shot at a critical moment in the game, *mental excitement* can no longer tie his swing up and he can make his shots normally even if his brain is befogged.

A good boxer will box on even when "out on his feet," and the good golfer should equally be able to produce his best shots even though he is five down with six to play. I had long realized the importance of this and the desirability of finding some way of *insulating* a golfer's shots from his mental state. I had worked out a very effective simple and satisfactory swing, but I did not know how to teach this except as a set of purely mechanical ideas.

But when I had developed the idea of control through remembered feeling, I was able to take the words "think" and "thought" out of my teaching vocabulary. The results were literally astounding.

And why? Not because I taught a better swing, but because my pupils learned to use their swings irrespective of conditions and states of mind! Many of my pupils now say, "I am no longer *afraid* of the ball. I do not even *think* of it; I just swing through it."

That, of course, means confidence and consistency.

On Learning Golf

What do these mean in results? Well, since I began teaching on these lines my pupils at St. Cloud included Mrs. A. M. Vagliano, two handicap, Captain of the Ladies' French International team; Mme Munier (*née* Jánine Gaveau), scratch, four times lady champion and International; the Duchesse d'Elkingen (*née* Mlle Francine Tollon), one handicap, twice lady champion and International; Mme Straus (*née* Aline de Gunsbourg), scratch, once lady champion French and International; Mme Decugis, two handicap, International; Mlle Petin, two handicap, International; the Comtesse de St. Sauveur (*née* Lally Vagliano), plus one, champion of France, International and British Girls Champion at seventeen.

All these ladies were gifted, intelligent, young, and keen, and they made teaching a pleasure. Also they were all under the golfing influence of the cool-headed player Mme Lacoste (*née* Simone Thion de la Chaume) of whose judgment I have the highest opinion. Her own game is the essence of perfect mental and physical balance.

But it is not only in molding the styles of the young and talented that the idea of control by remembered feel is so invaluable in the teaching of golf. One lady who came to me for her first lesson at the age of forty had the temerity to knock the great Mme Lacoste out of the French Championship ten years later!

Now here, for those who collect coincidences, is a true story which shows an independent and extremely

Golf and the Senses

practical application of the ideas on which my teaching is based.

I was giving a lesson to a young American, a thoughtful, analytical fellow who up to that time had taught himself all the games he had played. He came to me because he could not connect what he knew he *should* do at golf with the physical action of doing it. So as briefly as possible I explained to him the idea of control by remembered feel. He was deeply interested, for though he had taken a course in psychology at college he had not thought of golf as one of the interests in which a knowledge of the subject might help him. He saw the point, and when he had reflected on it told me this very curious story.

"When I first came to England, the traffic keeping to the left instead of to the right as it does back home nearly got me time after time. Whenever I was going to step off the sidewalk I looked to the left instead of to the right as I should have done.

"This got so dangerous that I had to take a dip into my brain-box to find a way of checking it. It wasn't any good just *telling* myself to look right; I had done that and promptly looked left again! So I decided that every time before stepping off a curb I would raise my right forearm and clench my fist. I reckoned it would draw my attention to the right as desired, *and it did*. In a few days I was cured."

Do you see the full significance of that story? Here was an intelligent fellow who knew that he *should*

On Learning Golf

look right before stepping off the curb, but who could not do it merely by knowing that he should do it, because he had been brought up to look left. Looking left had become a muscular memory with him, and in the control of actions, knowledge and thought can never equal muscular memory. Finding this so, this very intelligent young man decided to build up *a new muscular memory* with the sequence: edge of curb—raise right arm, clench fist—*look right.* And it worked.

Now here was a clear case of an effective psychological-physical control being developed out of the necessities of the moment with no formal knowledge of the concept whatever.

Exactly the same development has taken place in the game of every successful golfer.

CHAPTER III

Fundamentals

2. THE SWING

I HAVE already explained briefly why, both in my own game and in my teaching, I have adopted the simplest possible swing and have insisted that as many shots as possible should be played with fundamentally the same movements. Now that I have outlined the idea of teaching by feel you will better understand why I attach such importance to this point.

To put the lesson of the concept of control by feel as briefly as possible, we must give up *thinking* about our shots. In place of thinking there must be *conscious control*, obtained by building up (by constant repetition of the correct action) a comfortable and reliable *feel*, a feel that will tell you infallibly through appeal to your muscular memory, what is the right movement —and which will remain with you and control your shots whatever your mental state may be. Not being a matter of *thought*, this control stands outside the mental state.

As I have said, this controlling *feel* is built up through the constant repetition of the correct movements. We do not know just where in the system it resides, but whether it is muscular memory, or the wearing of certain grooves or channels in the mind,

On Learning Golf

or—as is probable—a combination of the two, it is obvious that the more often the same succession of movements can be repeated the clearer the memory will be. Also, and this is most important, it is highly desirable that the memory should not be confused by the frequent or even occasional introduction of other and different movements—as happens when the swing is fundamentally changed for certain shots.

It is mainly for this reason that I teach and preach and practice that every shot from the full drive to the putt should be played with the same movement. Of course in the drive the movement is both more extensive and bolder than for the shorter shots, but fundamentally it is the same. The result must be a feeling of "in-to-out" stroking across the face of the ball—played not at the ball, but through it. The "in-to-out" refers to the relation of the feel of the path of the club head to the desired line of flight of the ball.

The only shots in golf which I have been unable to play or to teach as sections of the fundamental "in-to-out" swing are certain shots which call for cut pulled under and across the ball.

But for ninety-nine out of every hundred shots a golfer must play, *the swing* is the movement necessary. So to clear the ground I will list what I consider to be the essentials of the swing:

1. It is essential to turn the body round to the right and then back and round to the left, without moving

The Swing

either way. In other words this turning movement must be from a fixed pivot.
2. It is essential to keep the arms at full stretch throughout the swing—through the back swing, the down swing, and the follow through.
3. It is essential to allow the wrists to break fully back at the top of the swing.
4. It is essential to delay the actual hitting of the ball until as late in the swing as possible.
5. It is essential not to tighten any muscle concerned in the reactive part of the swing (movement above the waist).
6. It is essential to feel and control the swing *as a whole* and not to concentrate upon any part of it.

In a sense this last point is the most vital. The swing must be considered and felt as a single unity, not as a succession of positions or even a succession of movements. *The swing is one and indivisible.*

Now I consider that our golf is liable to go wrong if we lose sight of any of these essentials. There are of course innumerable incidentals that could be added that are important enough to have a considerable influence on one's game, but I will go so far as to say that if you have these six essentials well embedded in your system and if you have developed some conscious control of your swing by getting the *feel* of the right movements—your game will rarely or never desert you.

Of course the comfortable, reliable, *right* feel is not a thing that comes all at once. For instance, it takes years—though not if your teacher teaches by feel—to

On Learning Golf

feel nicely set and comfortable before the ball; weight between the feet, perfectly free and active and yet firmly *planted*.

Then the waggle. About the waggle a whole book could be written. Every movement we make when we waggle is a miniature of the swing we intend to make. The club head moves in response to the body and the body opposes the club head. It is a flow and counter flow of forces with no static period, no check.

There is no check anywhere in a good swing. There is no such thing as the "dead top" of a swing—there are four points each one of which might be so considered if it were not for the other three! They are: (1) When the pivot (feet to shoulders) has reached *its* top, the arms are still going up. (2) When the arms have reached *their* top, the body is on its day down. (3) When the arms begin to come down, the wrists have still to break back, and (4) When the wrists break.

Now these four points together make up the top of the swing, and I was talking about the waggle—which is the bottom of an imaginary swing! But do not think I was digressing. I was not, the two are linked together. And why? Because unless you feel the whole of the swing in your waggle, your waggle is failing in its purpose.

The whole meaning and purpose of the waggle is that you shall first feel your swing rightly so that you may then make it rightly. I remember watching Sandy Herd makes his first Ciné pictures. In order not to

The Swing

waste film he tried to do without his customary fourteen waggles and in consequence he could not hit the ball. He could not make his shot because he had not *felt* it. They got over the difficulty eventually by letting him have his full fourteen waggles but only starting the camera at about number ten!

There is of course a great deal more to be said about the swing than I have said in this chapter, which is intended simply as an outline of the fundamentals as I see them. Much of the detail will be dealt with in later chapters.

NEARING THE TOP OF THE SWING

POINTS TO STUDY

The impression here is that the weight is being pushed against the left foot. It looks *inside*.

BELOW THE WAIST

The left knee has moved horizontally forward and around in a semicircle. Because this movement has been horizontal the left heel has been lifted.

The right leg is taut and nearly straight . . . not quite straight. The weight has remained central as at the address so the right leg is not vertical.

The hips are horizontal (like the knees). The right hip has not sagged or moved laterally; it has turned straight back.

ABOVE THE WAIST

The shoulders have turned horizontally to the spine.

Because of the upright stance—the spine being very little inclined forward—the shoulders have not dipped appreciably.

The left shoulder has not dipped, but it has come under and along to the chin.

The left arm is not stiff but it is straight, and the hands are held out as wide as possible.

This is the region of the *reverse*. The arms are near their top, but the wrists have still to break back fully as the left heel returns back to the ground.

NEARING THE TOP OF THE SWING

PERCY

CHAPTER IV

Golf Bogey No. 1

o

I HAVE christened it Golf Bogey No. 1 because it is the most seductive and destructive medium in the game. It took me most of the years of my golfing life to discover it and even then I could not formulate my ideas about it or counteract it effectively in my teaching until I had come to a proper understanding of the relation between the physical and mental in golf.

Now I can present it to you properly. Golf Bogey No. 1 *is the natural urge to act in the obvious way to achieve the desired result.*

The seductiveness of the idea is clear; its destructiveness lies in the fact that in golf (as in many other affairs in life) the obvious way is not always the right way. Frequently the obvious way is the *wrong* way and unless the urge to follow it can be *inhibited* the right way cannot be taken.

To use Professor Alexander's excellent phrase, the man who follows the obvious way is an *end gainer*. He is so keen and intent upon gaining his end (getting his ball onto the green and into the hole) that he concentrates upon *that* rather than upon the employment of what he knows to be the correct technique or the *means whereby* the end can best be gained. He is so

29

On Learning Golf

intent upon his end that he tries to take short cuts to it—or, to put it more accurately, he no longer remembers that it is necessary to go round by a certain road to get there.

That the *obvious* way is often in conflict with the *right* way in golf is clear on the slightest thought. The most effective swing is artificial rather than natural, and even more closely relative to our point—any experienced golfer knows that it is impossible to make a good drive when thinking of hitting the ball a certain distance in a certain direction on to the green.

But that is where it has to be hit, you say? Agreed. But the point is that it cannot be hit there with any certainty unless the end in view is inhibited—or at least made secondary—and the whole system is concentrated upon performing a proper *swing*, i.e. upon the reasoned means whereby the desired aim may be achieved. In short you must not think about and calculate distance and direction; you must *feel* the swing that will give you the desired distance and direction.

This may seem a simple point, but it is so basically important that I will illustrate it by relating the experience of one of my pupils.

I had in Paris a golf school where five or six assistants worked under my guidance. So most of my personal work was in perfecting the ground work which my assistants had built up in beginners, or in the more difficult and trying re-educational work for pupils who have got down to 6 or so and then stuck. It was one

Golf Bogey No. 1

of these re-educational cases which gave me an unusually clear revelation of the machinations of Golf Bogey No. 1.

The lady, an International golfer nearer fifty than forty years of age, was in a thoroughly bad patch. Her handicap was 3 but she could not play anywhere near it at the time. She came to me and asked me to "overhaul her swing." I asked if she realized what that meant and whether she would have the pluck and perseverance to carry through what might amount to a complete re-formation of a swing which had, when all was said, brought her considerable success. I suggested that she should think it over for a week.

During the week I inquired of her friends, who assured me that she was persevering and intelligent. I knew she was of good physique. That was enough for me, for though I did not feel that she had any great natural gift for the game, I knew that intelligence and perseverance were qualities which could call others to their aid. So I was willing to take the case on, and after thinking it over she decided that she would like me to take her in hand.

She proved to be a most delightful and receptive pupil and in a short time was sweeping the ball away magnificently with all her clubs. I admit that I began to think I was something of a teaching genius—and indeed my delighted pupil told me I was! But then came disaster.

Like all good mothers, my pupil took her children to

On Learning Golf

the mountains for the Winter Sports and being an all-round sportswoman—she is a good yachtswoman too—she tried a few easy slopes herself. I have never been on skis, and probably never shall, as I can't afford to risk my limbs, so I cannot say from personal experience how skiing *should* mix with golf—but I know how it did in this case! My pupil came back physically undamaged, fit as ever, mentally happy and untroubled, yet her swing—! *What* a mess! Completely slowed up, I told her.

As is my habit when things go seriously wrong, I began all over again: pivot, width, etc. Yet nothing happened except a further crop of half-tops, scoops, and all the lifeless, hopeless shots that a poor swing produces. In a sense, we both knew what was wrong without being able to cure it—we knew her club was coming down "outside" the ball every time. Yet to save her life my pupil could not prevent it!

So it went on until one day in what proved to be a moment of inspiration I said, "You seem to be trying to *guide* the ball down the middle."

"Well," she replied, "that is where you want me to hit it—isn't it?"

"If you insist on putting it that way—yes," I said. "But I would rather you felt that that is *where we want the ball to go,* not where we want you *to hit it.* Certainly you must not try directly to hit it down the middle, by making your club head take the line down the middle."

Golf Bogey No. 1

"But surely," she complained, "the ball goes where you feel the club head goes."

"By no means," said I. "From experience I know that unless I feel my club head goes out to the right my ball will *not* go down the middle—it will be pulled or horribly sliced. I know—by experience again—that if I want the ball to fly straight down the middle I must feel that I swing my club *not* in the direction of the hole, but at an angle to what I want to be the line of flight."

"Then you feel you swing your club in one direction to make the ball go in another?" she said.

"I do. And why? Because I could not be a good golfer if I did not!"

So much for the immediate cause of the trouble, but I wanted to dig deeper. Why had the trouble arisen? Before she went to the mountains my pupil was playing beautiful in-to-out shots—sweeping the ball away gloriously with every club. Why, oh why the breakdown?

We puzzled over it a great deal, but she could suggest no reason for it. But one day she said: "I do remember faintly that when you took me in hand first you *did* tell me to swing from in-to-out. You even sketched a line on the ground for me to follow.[1] But I did not realize that was fundamental—I thought it was a stunt of yours to cure some personal fault of mine."

[1] See Diagram on page 129.

On Learning Golf

I was angry! All that trouble because my pupil had taken me for a stunt merchant! Whatever I tell a pupil is *considered,* as are the phrases I tell it in. I told that pupil to swing the club head from in-to-out because that is an essential feel of good golf—and for no other reason. At least, all's well that ends well—and I am happy to say that since that day my pupil has never looked back.

What has that to do with Golf Bogey No. 1? Everything. We see the stimulus to put the ball near the flag ruining the lady's game—because she became so intent upon reaching that *end* that she overlooked the means whereby it might be achieved, the correct in-to-out swing that sends the ball down the desired line of flight.

CHAPTER V

The Road to Golfing Health

○

NOW I could write a whole book on the experience of my pupil briefly outlined in the preceding chapter. It might be made a very interesting book too, for the case contained all the elements of a perfect illustration of the desirability of some sort of *conscious* control that could be used to check the often fatal tendency to do the obvious thing. For do not forget it was Golf Bogey No. 1—the natural tendency to do the obvious thing—that upset my pupil's game.

As soon as she wilfully tried to drive down the middle of the fairway she was a mess. When she reverted to the proper method of *considering the stroke*, not the ball and *not* the distant green and tried to sling her club head out into the rough on her right—she became a beautiful, sweeping machine again. But note that we only arrived at this happy state when reason had dominated instinct—when her golf had evolved from instinctive end-gaining to *conscious control* of the stroke.

This conscious control, as I see it, can only be *built up* in some such manner as I have used in my teaching. Conscious control by *feel* certainly cannot be made use of simply by accepting its theoretical basis! Nor can

On Learning Golf

it be made use of by copying the style and swing of someone who possesses it! It has to be *built up* in the individual golfer. And how? My own method will be described in later chapters.

It may be timely to suggest here that the "conscious" in *conscious control* is a warning that a fine and experienced golfer is not *necessarily* a good teacher of the game. Why? Because many cracks do not know how they play themselves—when it comes to anything like a close analysis of their shots—and they have no idea at all of how a beginner must feel in order to make the shots that they make.

Let me illustrate that last point, because it is fundamental to teaching and to learning. All crack players feel that they swing from in-to-out when driving. I have been doing this so long that it no longer feels a "guided" or unnatural swing to me. Indeed if I feel myself making any other sort of swing I know it will result in a bad shot. Yet with the beginner this in-to-out swing does *feel* unnatural and gives an impression that the ball will be pushed into the rough to the right. This feeling will of couse be corrected by experience. This disparity in *feeling* about shots as between the crack and the beginner must never be lost sight of in teaching.

Every teacher has to keep continually in mind the fact that the natural thing for any golfer to do if he thinks first of hitting the ball to the hole rather than of making the shot correctly—is to swing the club head

The Road to Golfing Health

down the desired line of flight. The urge to do this is so strong that a merely academic knowledge of where the club head ought to be felt to go cannot stand against it. William James said that where there is a conflict between the Will and the Imagination, the Imagination *always* wins. So no Will to make a correct swing—unless reinforced by our conscious control—can resist, when imagination of the ball flying straight for the hole supervenes. What usually happens is that before the back swing is completed, the player *transfers his attention from the matter of making the correct swing to the matter of where he wants to hit the ball,* i.e., somewhere at the top of his swing he switches from a correct in-to-out swing to one along the desired line of flight. Consequently he comes down *outside the ball.*

Anyone who is not a pupil of mine will admit that "you came down outside" is their tutor's most frequent admonition. And why do I say, "who is not a pupil of mine?" Well because I never just tell them that! It is quite useless to tell a pupil he has done wrong when acting instinctively *unless you tell him why he did wrong* and so enable him to avoid the fault in future. That I always do.

The player who comes down outside is almost invariably thinking of where he wants to put the ball, and the only effective way of overcoming his trouble is by getting him to concentrate on the swing that experience tells him will *place* it there. If this is done

On Learning Golf

his conscious control—his feeling for the right movements, plus a steady intention to follow will inhibit his natural desire to take disastrous short cuts.

So Golf Bogey No. 1 can only be defeated by building up a swing which can be accepted by the mind as well as the muscles as a satisfactory means to the end desired, and then concentrating on the production of that swing. With a properly felt swing, *the swing becomes the aim* and the matter of where the ball will fly is left (as it should be) to take care of itself.

And finally, the good golfer feels his swing as *all one piece*. It is produced by a psycho-physical unison and its control is outside the mind of the player. Any control that is *within* the mind is subject to the state of the mind and is therefore unreliable.

Here we come back again to my reason for standardizing as many shots as possible so that they can all be played with the same set of "controls." Only so I believe can you learn to play entirely by sense of feel. Today, if I play a bad shot I do not start asking myself why I played it badly, what I did wrong, etc.—questions which are liable to lead to more bad shots as we all know! I just take an *easy* club and try it until I get the right feel again. Then because my shots are *felt* I know that the right feeling must lead to the right shot—and further, that as all my shots are made fundamentally the same, I know that if I get the right feel with say a No. 5 iron, a very easy club, I shall be mak-

The Road to Golfing Health

ing my shots with even the difficult clubs correctly and with confidence.

As I said before, these *controls* to which feeling a club gives the key, are probably in muscular memory *plus* tracks worn in the mind. But wherever they reside it is clear that the fewer there are of them the more reliable they are likely to be. If I play a pitch one way, a drive another, an iron shot in yet another, and a putt quite differently again, it is obvious that no single and consistent line of controls will be set up. Confusion as between one set of controls and another is very likely, and if I go off my game I may go off it very badly!

On the other hand if my system is used, a single sound line of controls *is* set up—by consistently practicing the same fundamental swing for every shot. Working on these lines and refusing to be side-tracked by extraneous ideas such as "hitting a long ball" or "driving straight down the middle," you can begin to feel a complete assurance that you can at least rely upon producing your best shots every time. They will become a *habit* with you.

CHAPTER VI

The Concentration Fallacy

○

IN whatever class of golf you play you will agree that the quality which enables the fellow just above you to give you strokes is not so much his ability to make shots which you cannot, as his knack of keeping his average shot nearer his best than you can. And this prime virtue of consistency is commonly credited to concentration.

And concentration is taken to mean such a pulling of oneself together, such a fixing of the mind on the task in hand, such a tight-lipped determination to do one's best, that golf becomes a trial of nervous strength rather than a game.

Now my own observation of many thousands of golfers from neophytes to tigers is that this form of concentration does *not* assist the production of one's best game. In fact I think the whole "concentration" doctrine a perversion of the truth, almost a reversal of it. I say that a golfer can only produce his true quality when he can play *without* concentrating (in this sense), when he can make his shots without clenching his teeth.

Nothing makes a simple physical action so difficult as does "concentration." Consider this odd fact about

The Concentration Fallacy

walking. We pay less attention to walking down a street than to walking over a plank across a stream—and *because* we pay less attention to it we walk at least as straight and with much better balance, greater firmness, and greater ease.

Simply because the penalties of deviating from the straight are so much greater when crossing the plank, we feel we have to concentrate our attention on the job. And it is this attitude of over-tense attention that makes the simple and familiar act of walking straight so suddenly and curiously difficult.

Now we can translate that directly into a common golfing experience. Put the average good golfer on a tee with a fairway fifty yards wide before him, and time after time he will drive slap down the middle of it. Yet reduce the width of that fairway to fifteen yards and he will become so conscious of its narrowness—so concentrated on the importance of keeping dead straight—that time after time he will put himself well out in the rough. That is why a course with wide fairways is commonly more popular than a narrow one; the average golfer feels more comfortable about it and *because* he feels more comfortable, plays better.

Hitting a golf ball is not difficult, nor is walking straight, *so long as the penalties of failure are not great*. But introduce the plank bridge or the narrow fairway and the difficulties follow.

The desire to *guide the ball* dead straight increases with the need for a dead straight drive and the greater

On Learning Golf

the desire the greater the difficulty! So when we stand on a tee with a narrow fairway before us, we must use our will power to inhibit the desire to *guide* the ball and simply perform the swing which our golfing sense tells us will send the ball straight. In fact we must forget that the plank is a bridge and simply walk across it!

This is true about the longest shot in golf, the drive; it is equally true and even more obvious about the shortest, the putt. What a simple operation is the five-foot putt on a good green *when there is nothing hanging to it*—and how exasperatingly difficult when it will decide the hole, the match and the half-crown!

So I repeat that if concentration means focusing all our mental attention and capacity on the problems and penalties of the shot in hand, then concentration is destructive of good golf. Good golf, consistent golf, depends upon being able to shut out our mental machinery (with its knowledge of the difficulties of the shot, the state of the game, etc.) *from those parts of us which play golf shots.*

Our conscious mental machinery is obsessed by the problems of getting the ball up to the hole and into the hole. Our golfing self should be concerned with something quite different, with the movements necessary to produce a good shot. These movements are controlled by remembered feel and the only concentrating we must do is in guarding this "remembered feel" from interference.

The Concentration Fallacy

That is why when a match grows to a climax the great player is apt to become slower and slower. It is not that the putt on the last green is more difficult than that on the first; probably his experienced eye tells him all he needs to know about it at first glance. But he potters about, sometimes to the annoyance of uninitiated spectators, *until he has pushed all that the putt means out of his mind,* until all he is conscious of is the *feel* of the stroke that will hole the ball. Then, and not until then, he can hole it.

If you want my idea of the ideal mental attitude to the game I will give it you in two words—Walter Hagen's! Walter Hagen was not only one of the greatest golfers, he was one of the most buoyant. Wherever he played he simply oozed with the joy of life. The more he was up against it the better he played. He really enjoyed a fight and the harder it was the more superb his confidence.

The general verdict is that the Hage had a "marvellous temperament for the game." And what do we mean by that? My own interpretation is that the Hage had perfect psycho-physical equilibrium, that his mind and body were perfectly balanced and perfectly correlated for the purpose of the game of golf.

Walter Hagen had found by trial and error, as most of us do, how he could best hit the ball. He had got the *feel* of his shots thoroughly into his system and could pull them out whenever he wanted. While he was playing he inhibited any extraneous matters in

On Learning Golf

the most effective way possible—*he refused to let them into that part of himself that was concerned with his golf*. So he could play his best in circumstances that would have turned gray the hair of any less perfectly adjusted player.

Please note that the Hage did *not* concentrate in the accepted sense. He did not shut extraneous matters out of his mind; he merely shut them out of his golf. While he was playing he would talk intelligently about any subject that cropped up, stocks and shares, eating and drinking, politics or puritanism. *Nothing*, neither wind nor weather, bad greens, tight corners, or unduly chatty opponents, ever made the Hage *tense*. Consequently golf never exhausted him; he was as fresh at the end of a Championship as he was at its beginning.

Incidentally this mental limberness was not left behind on the last green. I remember talking to him at Sandwich on the day he won the British Open. He had finished and we sat and chatted for a long time while waiting to see if George Duncan would deprive him of the title which otherwise he had won. Well George very nearly did it, but Walter Hagen never batted an eyelid. He was as chatty, as cheerful, and as untense as ever—at the end of a week's competitive golf with the whole issue of a three thousand mile trip in the balance.

I suppose everyone would agree that "self-control" as effective as that possessed by men like Hagen and

The Concentration Fallacy

Harry Vardon is a priceless quality. But how achieve it? It can only be done by building one's golf into a closed, self-controlling circle, and then keeping extraneous matters outside that circle.

The reason why the neophyte and the player needing re-education find control so elusive is simply that *their* golf has not yet been built into such a closed circle. And if they only knew it they make things far worse by trying to *learn* golf and *play* golf at the same time. When that happens, pity the poor teacher!

The pupil, let us say, is making good progress. He is beginning to co-ordinate his game and build up his controls, when he suddenly takes himself off for an afternoon in an entirely different atmosphere—that of competitive golf, in which *style* means nothing and immediate results everything. Of course his budding style and incipient control go overboard and *end-gaining* dominates. Everything is subordinate to getting the ball into the hole, so Golf Bogey No. 1 wins again. It is only an intentionally established set of controls that can resist the temptation to *force* and *guide* the ball when much is at stake.

These controls are the thing! Their creation and development must be the constant aim of both pupil and teacher. Everything helping their development must be encouraged, everything hindering it avoided. Their building up is largely unconscious and unnoticed, indeed even a successful pupil will often feel that little progress is being made—until perhaps quite suddenly

On Learning Golf

he will be surprised to find himself playing effective, confident golf.

I remember with special pleasure how that happened to a young pupil of mine, Mlle Aline de Gunsbourg. She had been in my hands since her childhood and her first experience of a major tournament was when she went over to England for the Ladies' Open. *She actually led the field in the qualifying rounds* and was only put out on the last green in the semi-final by Pam Barton, the eventual winner.

On her return she said to me, "I did not know I could play like that! No one was more surprised than I was. I just played—and everything went right."

I was delighted, but not so surprised. I knew she had the golf in her and that sooner or later the controls we were building would enable her to play it. But I was delighted, because you would not normally expect a young pupil to play a bit above her best on such a nerve-testing occasion.

So when a golfer says to me, "I must learn to concentrate—concentrate—concentrate!" I counter with: "No, you must build controls—controls—controls!"

Part Two

ON LEARNING AND TEACHING

o

BEFORE we go ahead with the next chapter, which is the first dealing with the practical side of learning to play golf, I want to say a few things about learning the game and about teaching it. I ought to know something about these subjects for I have been learning golf for forty-five years—and teaching it as well for the last thirty of them.

Now I claim that the right way of learning golf has almost nothing in common with the "learning" we did at school; it is an entirely different process. Memorizing the capitals of Europe or a Latin declension, or "learning" chemistry or mathematics, are purely mental feats and depend exclusively upon *mental memory*, whereas I contend that to learn to play good and consistent golf you need *muscular memory*.

What you need to learn (or memorize) are not the technical or mathematical details of a good shot but *the feel of it*. If you and every component muscle in you can remember the feel of a good shot, *you can make it*—and you have become what I term a reflex golfer. That is to say, the good shot has become your "reflex," or *automatic response* to the sight of the ball. But please remember that this golf memory is *a memory of a cycle of sensations* which follow and blend into one another quite smoothly. Each sensation must be connected up with those which precede and follow it;

On Learning Golf

it cannot be considered independently. The truth is that it cannot even be *felt* independently. You cannot, to take a crude example, *feel* the top of your swing as such; you can only feel a sensation between the sensations of the back swing and those of the down swing.

For that reason you must never in golf say, "I've got it!" when you think you have found the secret of some shot that has been evading you—unless what you have "got" fits into your cycle of sensations or, as we shall now call them, *controls*. Because, unless it does so fit in, it cannot become a reliable part of your game. And why do I call sensations controls? Simply because I want you to control your golf by these sensations instead of by *thought*.

There is another reason why your memory of a golf shot must be a memory of a cycle of sensations, not of a number of separate sensations. It takes an exceedingly skilful juggler to juggle with six glass balls at once, but if the six balls were threaded onto a string most of us could manage them—and the memorizing of sensations as a cycle (instead of as independent items) does *thread them up* for us very much in this way.

To turn for a moment from learning to teaching. Most of the teaching of golf is completely negative—and a purely negative thing can have no positive value. Why do I say that golf teaching is negative? Well we can all find faults in each other's game, millions of them, and we all start off to teach golf by pointing out

On Learning and Teaching

these faults and "curing" them. I did this for twenty-five years, but I have now discovered that the right way to get a pupil to hit the ball satisfactorily is *to watch for any good natural qualities* that may be there and to build up the swing around them.

We all hit a good ball sometimes. Maybe with the beginner this is an accident, but the good teacher will use such an accidental shot, photographing it in his mind and starting away to build up controls around the qualities which made it possible.

In this way the beginner can retain his natural capacity to hit the ball and will gain confidence in his ability to do it—and so go on enjoying his game and improving it. But if the teacher merely points out to him a dozen or more faults in his swing he will become perplexed, confused, and fed up. For that reason I never tell a pupil his faults (which is negative teaching). I notice the faults, of course, *and suggest the necessary corrections* (which is positive). So I never tell a pupil that he overswings and breaks his left arm, I explain width to him. That is to say I give him a positive conception and by working on it he actually cures his faults without even being aware that he had them.

Now there is another point about teaching which I would like to emphasize. You will find that in this work I have not tried to set down a set of controls in one way and leave it at that. I have tried to set the same things down and explain them in many different ways. So when you find me repeating myself do not think it is

On Learning Golf

carelessness! All good teachers must repeat, but never in exactly the same words or with just the same connections. I want to give you a clear idea of the controls which will enable you to produce an effective swing, and I do not mind if I have to say the same thing in a dozen different ways so long as one of the twelve gets home with you. I hope you will not mind either, because you should be able to pick something new out of the other eleven also.

I learned golf by the long way—trial and error—and I want to lead you away from that to a method which is methodical and is effective whatever your age or your handicap may be. If you accept my method of learning you do not need a lot of practice on the course to improve; you can assimilate the principles in your armchair and put in useful practice on the hearth rug—where you need no club because you can *feel* your muscular movements without it. You must learn to feel the sensations through your intellect and then forget them intellectually and leave them to your muscular memory or control system.

How long does it take to "learn golf"? Well I am still learning after forty-five years of it! I have known pupils who hit the ball very well after only four lessons and others who have taken a year or more to do even moderately well, but time is apt to level things out a lot. Golf is a curious game in being easy of comprehension but (sometimes) very long in realization. There is much darkness in the early stages, and it is only after

On Learning and Teaching

a few years at the game that we really come out into full daylight and can assess our own possibilities.

Early difficulties are often emphasized by age or physical make-up. While I was writing this I had just started two young ladies—one of sixteen who is still at college but weighs about one hundred and seventy pounds and another in the early twenties who weighs less than half that. Apart from the weight of their clubs the conditions will be the same for both, yet obviously their problems will work out very differently. And we have all got our physical individuality and peculiarities in the layout of bones and development of muscles. But I have found by long experience that these things usually level themselves out in the end—I have seen many gifted and precocious beginners fail simply because they would not put in the hard work which is essential before the elementary stage is passed, and only when the elementary stage is passed can golf genius come to the surface.

On the other hand I remember one pupil of mine who started very young and at times could hardly get the ball off the ground; yet at eighteen she was scratch and Champion of France. And as I have already told, I started another lady at forty and though she was not gifted she was a worker and ten years later she eliminated Mme Lacoste from the French Open!

So do not despair if you are trying to learn golf, or better golf, and getting no results. It may be that you have been trying to learn too many things (like jug-

On Learning Golf

gling with too many balls) and when you have tried to add just one more, your whole game has broken down on you. We will simplify the things you have to learn by stringing them together into cycles of sensation because they are then easier to remember and easier to *add to*.

If you work in this way your golf will be *progressive*. You will still (being human) get bad patches, but each bad patch will tend to be less bad and each good patch will tend to be better, because you are *building up* your game.

The foundation upon which it must be built up is the *feel of the swing;* so in the first practical chapter I give you an idea of the whole swing—just as I do in the first lesson when personal teaching is possible.

The subsequent chapters are what a musician might call "Variations on the Theme!" Hence the apparent repetition. Because I believe that all golf shots should be made with the same controls, you will not find anything fundamentally different in the chapter on Putting than that which you will find in the chapter on the Full Swing. Yet you might quite possibly get a control for your driving out of the Putting chapter; it depends on your make-up and on what you read into what I have written.

Some years ago I told a pupil, in the course of a lesson, "I drive as I putt." Three years later he said to me, "You once told me you drove as you putted—what you meant was that you putted as you drove." I let him

On Learning and Teaching

have his own way! The great thing was that we had got the two associated in his mind and controls and so proved my system to be teachable and workable in others. I have had plenty of confirmation of this since.

In finishing this chapter I will return again to the need to make your learning *positive*. Don't go out to find out what is wrong with your swing, go out to improve it. You will be none the worse if you start with a really big idea—to learn (or re-learn) the golf swing at your first try. If that is your ambition do not tie yourself up with theories; stand up and give the ball a crack—that is the most positive thing in golf.

CHAPTER VII

The Controlled Golf Swing

AS you have already heard, my first endeavor is to teach the pupil the whole golf swing—or better, the golf swing as a whole. I do not believe in trying to impart the swing in stages or by sections; from the first lesson I teach the swing complete.

What the pupil gets from this first lesson is a *grosso modo* idea of how the swing works; what I get from it is mainly an indication of how the *grosso modo* strikes the pupil as an individual. For do not forget that whatever I say and however I illustrate my points, *every pupil will visualize the swing differently.*

I had a heartbreaking experience of this early in my teaching days when I had to take classes, twenty pupils at a time. All the twenty heard and saw the same things, but the extraordinary interpretations some of the individuals put on them were astounding. I could not stand it and gave the job up. The trouble in writing about the game is that I realize that in a sense my readers are a class. So I must take endless trouble to insure that you shall understand what I write.

Now for our *grosso modo* exposition of how the swing works.

The beginning of the movement is in the feet; the

The Controlled Golf Swing

movement passes progressively up through the body, through the arms, and out at the club head. What we try to do is to make the club head come down in the same path time and time again—in such a way that the face of the club comes squarely into the back of the ball every time. We have one fixed point (the feet) and one moving point (the club head) which we desire to move along the same line time after time. So the golf swing might be compared to the drawing of arcs with a pair of compasses. The reasons why we cannot be so precise in our stroking as the compass can, are that *we* are supported on two legs instead of one and we are full of flections and joints!

Again, we have not only to bring the club head down through the same line time after time; we must bring it down so that the club face is square with the ball at the instant of impact—and because the path of the club head is a curve, this means that impact must be *timed* correctly to an infinitesimal fraction of a second in the sweep of the swing. Also the club head must be *accelerating* at the moment of impact.

So we have not only to set up the mechanism to make a good swing, which we can all soon do if we only swing at the daisies, but we have to *time* this swing to the fraction of a second. Now I think that most of us overrate the value of good mechanics in golf and underrate the value of accurate timing. I was once watching, with a pupil of mine who had a most perfect swing, a fellow whose action was not pretty—to put it

On Learning Golf

kindly. But he kept hitting nice long shots down the middle. "Not much to look at," I remarked to my pupil. "I would not care a damn what I looked like if I could repeat like that chap!" he replied.

The awkward one *could* repeat his best shots time after time. His mechanics were ungainly but his timing was near perfect.

Well, you may say, if that is so, why should you go to so much trouble to give us a good mechanical swing? The answer is that good timing plus a good swing is better than good timing plus an awkward swing. The best swing, mechanically, is the one that pulls the ball a little and then makes it turn a bit to the left at the end of its flight, but if you get your maximum golf happiness out of a swing which slices the ball all around the course, there is no reason to alter your mechanics!

If you do want to make an alteration, it may not be an extensive one. I remember one day at St. Cloud an American came and begged me to give him even fifteen minutes—which I did out of my lunch time as he seemed so insistent.

His trouble was that every now and then his iron shots to the green would finish in the bunker to the left of the green. For three years he had failed to find a permanent cure. So on the advice of a friend he came to me. It did not take me long to see what was wrong and to explain to him that now and again his foot-and-leg work was sluggish, and in consequence the club head came in too soon—to put his ball a little to the left.

The Controlled Golf Swing

After that brief lesson I never saw him again, as he was on his way back to the States from Paris. But he left me a note of thanks and a handsome present, and when I inquired of the caddy who had been out with him in the afternoon learned he had broken 70. Some time later I saw his photograph in the *American Golfer* with the news that he had won the West Coast championship.

Too much thought about the mechanics is a bad thing for anyone's game. Now the reason why golf is so difficult is that you have to learn it and play it *through your senses*. You must be mindful but not thoughtful as you swing. You must not think or reflect; you must *feel* what you have to do. Part of the difficulty arises because, apart from simple things like riding a bicycle, we have never learned to do things in this way.

The most difficult thing about learning golf is to learn to distract your mind from everything except the feeling of what you are about to perform.

Now no teacher can *tell* you in exact words how it feels when you make a certain movement correctly. You will have to use your imagination to interpret what he says, and if he is wise he will encourage you to use it.

Let me give you an example. I want to teach you to pivot from the hips. Now I can show you how it is done and issue the usual mass of detailed instruction, but that does not call up your imagination and it gives you no conception of how it *feels* to pivot correctly.

So, instead of explaining all the mechanical and an-

On Learning Golf

atomical details of the pivot to you, I show you how to pivot and then tell you to do it yourself *imagining that you are standing in a barrel hip high and big enough to be just free of each hip but a close enough fit to allow no movement except the pivot.* At once you get the *feeling* of the pivot. Incidentally nine out of ten golfers would improve their games if they would use this image to the fullest degree in practice.

So far so good; we can learn to feel the body turn to the right and round to the left, beautifully fixed in space by the hips. Now carry the image a stage further: first, as you pivot *sink down from the knees*—you will feel that if you sink down, even ever so little, you will become stuck in the barrel. *This will not do,* so you must feel that you keep your hips *up* on a level with the top of the barrel. Do this and you will develop the feel of keeping your hips up as you pivot—a thing which unfortunately for our golf very few of us do.

Now do not think that we use *imagination* in teaching golf in order to evolve new theories. Oh no—there are too many theories already! What we use imagination for is to translate theory into *feeling*, and to keep our minds awake and our circle of golfing sensations expanding. Every new golfing sensation (if it is to be deliberately induced and not left to happen by accident) may need an introduction through the imagination in this way—but once the image has done its work of introduction it can be put on one side and the *feel* that it has made known can be relied on. But put your

The Controlled Golf Swing

images on one side—do not abandon them, because if you *do* lose the feel, the image through which you learned it will bring it back.

Now the golf swing is a connected series of sensations or feels and when you get all these *feels* right and rightly connected you will swing perfectly. I have just given you the *feel* of the pivot—the movement on which the modern swing is based.

Now to that one basic feel, the pivot, we will add other feels, and every new feel gives you a new *control* until your whole game is controlled and you can play it as you will. But do not think you cannot play until you have this whole series of controls established. Lots of players go through their golfing lives and get a lot of fun out of the game without building up any controls at all! But the more controls you can build up *and link together*, the better for your game, the finer the conception of the swing you will evolve.

Let us get back to the visualizing of our swing. We have laid our foundation by getting the *feel* of the pivot from the hips. This movement goes up through the body to the next control point—the shoulders. And here I believe that wrong imagination does a great deal of damage to many people's swings.

We think that in the fine swing we see the left shoulder come down as we come back and the right shoulder come down as we come forward; so we feel that this shoulder movement is *right* and tend to encourage it—to the detriment of our swings because it is *wrong*. And

On Learning Golf

I say it is wrong, cheerfully certain that it *is* wrong in spite of its almost universal acceptance. How much the shoulders actually dip depends upon how erect we stand when addressing the ball. We should stand as erect as possible and I contend that we should *not* feel our shoulders go down but should feel that we are keeping them fully up.

As we address the ball we look at it a little sideways —we *peep* at it. The head is fixed (because you "keep your eye on the ball"), and the movement of the shoulders is not an independent movement of the shoulders at all, but is due to the shoulders *being moved around from the pivot*. We can only keep the shoulder movement in a fixed groove and make it *repeatable* time after time, by keeping the shoulders at the limit of *upness* in whatever position the turn from the hips may have placed them. Any *excess* of upness (that is, actual shoulder lift) will result in the ball being lost sight of. In short, the fixed head determines the limit of lift and dip of the shoulders.

You will see that this is why you must feel you keep the shoulders up to the same degree with, say, a driver and a full swing and a mashie niblick (a more upright club) and a half swing. The closer you stand to your ball the more upright the swing and the more directly downward your sight of the ball . . . also, the less extensive the swing you can make without losing sight of the ball.

Now try this conception of the shoulder action with-

The Controlled Golf Swing

out a club, and *link it to your feel of the pivot from the hips*. Feel how the two become connected. This is the first connection in our building up of a controlled swing—and a very important one. You cannot take too much trouble in understanding it and building it up.

From the shoulders our power travels down through the arms, and as to arm action also I believe the common conception to be erroneous. Most people think they lift their arms to get them to the top of the back swing. With a modern controlled swing they do *not* lift them . . . the arms work absolutely subjectively to the shoulders, that is why they *are* controlled.

But, you may say, if I do not lift my arms how do I get them up to the top of my swing? To find the answer, think this out. As you stand to the ball with the wrists slightly up, there is a straight line practically from the club head up the shaft and along your arm to the left shoulder, and as your hands are already waist high it needs only the inclining of the shoulders as we turn (on the pivot) to bring them *shoulder high*, without having altered their relative positions at all. They have not been *lifted;* they have gone up in response to the shoulder movement. This accounts for the curtailment *and* the control of the modern swing.

Naturally, the more flexible we are the more we can get our hands *up* without breaking up this connection, that is, without moving the arms independently. The triangle formed by our arms and a line between the shoulders should never lose its shape . . . it should be

On Learning Golf

possible to push a wooden snooker triangle in between the arms and to leave it there without impeding the swing back or through.

Now to my mind the foregoing are the three basic *feels* of the golf swing—the pivot, the shoulders moving in response to the pivot, and the arms moving in response to the shoulders. These are the basic movements of a connected and therefore *controlled* swing, and they must all be built into the framework of your *feel* of the swing.

Of course there are many additional nuances and supplementary *feels* which you will build up and recognize as your game develops, but though you will *add* to these three fundamentals you will never alter them. Therein lies much of their value. You will get used to taking a sly look at them occasionally as you go round the course, and so long as you keep these three primary *feels* right, nothing much will go wrong with your game.

And if your game does go wrong, if the shots which you thought you had mastered desert you, all you need to do is to go back to the *feel* of these three basic points. You just take a peep back at them, and then with one or two shots your mechanism will feel familiar again—and all the other supplementary feels which you have built up by practice will be enticed back.

Now we might break off this chapter at this point. I realize that I have already given you plenty to think of and to work at. But there is a development in your

The Controlled Golf Swing

game or in your way of playing it that I want to prepare you for; so, for that reason and for the sake of analyzing the matter out to its logical conclusion I add the following.

After a while by dint of pivoting correctly, not dipping our shoulders (i.e. *not* lifting with the arms), we begin to play some good shots, nice and straight and reasonably long. We have arrived at this stage by building on the basic trinity—pivot, shoulders up, and width—and by occasionally taking a sly peep at how they are going. *So far we have never consciously produced a good shot;* we have merely made certain mechanical movements which we have been taught will result in good shots.

But now we begin to realize how we should feel in order to produce a good shot. We are on the other side of the fence. We know now what it feels like to produce a good shot, and now, instead of preparing for a shot by sly looks at our pivot etc., we instinctively get into the position which we feel will produce a good shot. And as we go on, the *feeling* of this preparatory state comes more and more into the foreground.

Also because we are working from a secure basis we can now begin to notice the nuances and subtleties. We find that we produce purer shots from one sensation than from another only slightly different. We are enticed to arrange our back swing according to the type of shot we wish to produce: an extra pivot if we wish to pull or a restricted pivot if we wish to slice. But

On Learning Golf

please notice that this will not be a conscious, mechanical control—you will not say to yourself, "I wish to slice slightly so I will restrict my swing to an arc of so many degrees," you will simply alter your swing unconsciously in response to your *feeling* of what will produce the shot you want.

In other words, the control of your shots has now been placed outside your *conscious mind and will*. You have built up a feel that a certain swing will produce a slice—so you can produce a slice by getting that feel into your swing. This is only the beginning of control by feel to the very good golfer. He begins to hit a variety of shots, with little difference in flight or character and yet each subtly different and with its individual feel. He files away in the "feel cabinet" in his unconscious memory all these subtleties. Consequently he never has to "think out" a shot on the course—he sees the lie and the flight required, and these produce, by an automatic response, the right feel from his cabinet and so the right shot from his club.

In this connection consider the hanging lie. Now this golfer's bugbear is a bugbear simply because it is *thought* that a shot from a hanging lie must be difficult; so the very sight of such a lie *produces* difficulties in the mind. If you learn to play by *feel*, no such difficulties will crop up; the sight of a hanging lie will suggest the feel of the necessary swing, restricted and slightly from the outside with the face somewhat open in consequence. Because of the lie you feel that this will give

The Controlled Golf Swing

you a shot of normal height, though you feel (correctly again) that such a swing played on the tee would produce nothing better than a vulgar slice!

In one sense, when I tell a pupil at his own request how to play from a hanging lie, I am telling him something I do not know. All I know is the *feel* of how to play off a hanging lie—and I know that well, for when I was at my apex as a golfer I missed fewer shots from indifferent lies than I did from the tee—probably because I concentrated more severely on the difficult shots than on the easy ones. Difficulties help concentration. I would rather have a bunker to pitch over than a plain run up of the same distance to play.

I hope that this chapter is easier to read than it was to write. I like it as well as any in the book, because it does condense what I take to be the essence of the golf swing into a reasonable space, readable in a reasonable time, so that the beginning should not be forgotten before the end is reached. But it is a vast field to cover and much compression had to be exercised—so it might be as well if you turned back now and read it again!

CHAPTER VIII

Preparatory to the Swing

○

THE experienced eye can make a very accurate guess at the handicap of a player after seeing him make a few practice swings, and as soon as his address is completed we can be *sure* of his quality.

Now at first glance it might seem that it would be simple enough for anyone to learn to stand correctly before the ball—to cultivate an impressive address. Yet there *is* this difference which enables the cognizant to recognize even the subtle variation between the good and the very good golfer before the ball has been struck.

It is an interesting point and one of some practical importance, because it is *directly related to the true aim and purpose of the preparatory movements*. We can recognize a golfer's quality in these movements because they express both *what* he intends to do and *how* he intends to do it. The difference between the good and the ordinary golfer is that the good one *feels his shot through his address*.

Whether or not he has learned deliberately to play by feel, the good player feels, through his carriage and balance as he addresses the ball, the coming movement that will bring his club face squarely against the

Preparatory to the Swing

ball. Briefly to analyze the feeling of carriage and balance—he feels he is set inwards and behind the back of the ball and his legs, hips and shoulders are all *braced, inside and behind the ball.*

Now this is a point where I must ask you to stop and consider and analyze carefully exactly the meaning I want to convey by the word *braced* because this is most important to a realization of the correct *feel of the body.*

My dictionary defines a brace as "anything that draws together and holds tightly," and I think that is clear and that it expresses the feeling we have when we are *braced.* But you may try it and promptly come back with the question, "But how can I feel *braced* and yet not become *stiff?*" A very pertinent question, and I will try and give you the answer.

When we take lessons in deportment we are told to walk *with our hips pulled in,* in other words to brace our hips. Yet we know that this does not make our carriage stiff; it makes it not stiff but firm and decisive.

So also, when I tell you as you address the ball to keep your elbows close together, you will immediately feel a sensation of drawing in your elbows the one towards the other. As a consequence your arms will not feel like two separate and independent arms but like a linked united *pair* of arms; yet *they will not feel stiff.* The "holding together" of your shoulder blades holds the top of your structure together and links up with the power from your hips. You will find your biceps being

On Learning Golf

pulled into your thorax, your shoulders and arms being drawn together, and, if then the stomach is drawn inward, one definite (inward) *direction* of brace is set up.

The second direction in which we brace our bodies at the approach is *upwards,* yes upwards, towards the sky! The natural tendency as we stand to our ball is to droop from our hips and curve our backs. But if we are good golfers we resist this tendency by an *upward brace*—slightly bent over but pulled up to our full height and neither drooped nor curved.

Set like this we will feel our left side as straight as a poker, though not as stiff as one, and *our left foot pushing down into the ground.* Of course as the weight is equally divided between the feet, this *pushing down* is a feeling in the right foot also. The result is a highly desirable one; as a reaction to our upward brace, we feel ourselves *standing firm* as we address the ball—a thing we are frequently told to do but rarely told *how* to do!

So with our hips, shoulders, and arms braced and the body stretched upwards and braced, we no longer feel a loose, flabby, drooping figure but an upright and yet compact one. But we have one more direction of brace to add—this comes from the hips and I can best describe it as a twist forward which completes the bracing up of the whole body at the address.

As we stand to the ball our feet must not be too wide apart; the right foot should be at right angles to the

Preparatory to the Swing

line of flight, the left one pointed slightly out; a line across the toes of both feet should (like the line between the shoulders) be parallel to the line of flight. From this position, we twist our hips round (horizontally) to the left, not as far as they will go but as far as they can go in comfort, i.e., without pulling our hips out of shape. How far this is depends on how supple we are. Probably the degree of movement will be only slight, but the effect of this forward leftward twist is to tauten up the whole body without stiffening it.

Because we are anchored, first by our feet to the ground and secondly by our square-set shoulders held up against the forward pull of the hips, the right knee does not resist so we find our left side straight and our right side *bowed* inwards. And these, left side straight and right side bowed in, are very definite *feels* which come from (and can be used to check) correct bracing.

These three directions of brace should now make us feel a complete unit, which we can think of as "the set." I think they are what makes the good golfer feel *compact*. They give the feeling that we can carry the club head back away from the ball by the body twist *inwards* and behind the back of the ball. In other words, if you are properly braced there will be no sensation of wanting to *lift the club head up*. This is important; we should never feel that we lift the club head, but that we carry it back around with the body and along the ground.

This feeling that the club head keeps down is

On Learning Golf

equally necessary in the follow through, after we have sent the ball on its way. We must feel that we have dispatched the ball out and along but not up.

A pupil of mine once asked me, "But when my hands are *up* must they feel down?" My reply was, "Yes"—because the *down* feeling is not a feeling of position but of *direction of pull*. We call it that because it is most noticeable in two *downward* phases, (1) as we address the ball, and (2) at the moment of impact with it.

We are frequently and wrongly told to keep our left arm straight, when we should be told to aim for the feeling of it being *down*. If we look for that, our arm will be practically straight even at the top of our swing, because we are stretching it to obtain the *down* feeling. This is the reliable way of reaching this end, because it is conditioned and controlled by *feel* not thought. Incidentally this explains why you can be a top class golfer even if your left arm is not straight at the top of your swing—not the straightness but the *downness* is the vital factor.

Now I hope you see the reason for adopting the set before the ball which I have been describing. It is so that you will feel that you will bring the club face square into the back of the ball, not from above but from behind it. When I say that I putt as I drive, I simply mean that when I putt I feel that I roll the ball along from behind—and I feel the drive is only an

Preparatory to the Swing

enlargement of this sensation, not something different from it.

"One sensation for all shots." I keep harping on this because it is not the knowledge of what we have to do which leaves us on the course—it is the *feel* of what we want to do that is apt to evaporate unless we have built up a secure feel-memory of how the swing operates. The only way in which we can *repeat* correct shots time after time (and this is the greatest of golfing assets) is to be able to repeat the correct feel of how they are produced. This feel must begin right as well as continue and finish right, and that is why I have gone into such detail in the apparently simple matter of standing in front of the ball.

Now I do not suggest that you will get this properly braced feeling at once, or that you cannot play good golf until you do get it. My experience is that few beginners brace well, except mechanically. One pupil of mine who had made marvellous progress only fully realized the conception of bracing after two years—when he was already capable of an occasional 78. We knew, when he did realize it, that the 78's would now become more frequent because he would begin to repeat his best shots more often.

It is always a pleasure to teach intelligent analytically-minded players who think about their game, even if they are physically not capable of playing high-class golf. I remember a lady whose game had been largely

THE ADDRESS

POINTS TO STUDY

The stance is firm, compact, and braced, qualities essential to a fast swinger.

Note the triangle formed by the two arms and the shoulders.

Although the right wrist is held arched (that is, *up*), the right elbow is held in and down.

Note the inclination of the shoulders, due to the left side being straight and the right side curved.

The right elbow is *inside* the right hip.

The left arm and club are in line.

The shoulders and feet are square to the line of flight, the hips are profiled—that is, are at a slight angle to it.

The view of the ball from this position is a peeping at the back of the ball out of the left eye.

THE ADDRESS

AUBREY

Preparatory to the Swing

messed up because to "cure" a somewhat persistent slice someone had told her to draw her right foot back a bit and hold her right hip back. Well, I squared up her stance and showed her how to brace and she began sweeping the ball away so perfectly that she could hardly believe her eyes! The next day she came back and told me she had thought over what I had told her and had found a curious resemblance between my "hip brace" and something that Miss Irene Castle the dancer had said to her some years before.

"Do you know," she said, "that while studying the dancing of Egyptians from old illustrations, Miss Castle found that they did not dance with their feet and hips and shoulders square, but with the hips profiled to the other two lines, and Miss Castle put down much of her success as a dancer to the fact that she adopted this idea?"

Now that was exceedingly interesting to me, even if it *did* upset some of the reasons I had worked out for the hips being "profiled" at golf. Like most of those who had been lucky enough to see Miss Castle dance, I had wondered how she did it—and here was part of the answer. I am more than ever convinced that the correct bracing of the body in this way is as essential to good golf as it is helpful to good dancing and that it is something that we should all seek for whatever our caliber.

I remember playing with Lord Derby and, because of his rotund figure, reminding him of the old Scotch

On Learning Golf

golf adage I had heard from Sandy Herd when I was a boy. "Pull in your tummy, my Lord," I said. He looked at me and smiled. "Do you think I am Miss Wethered?" he said! At that time Miss Wethered was a slim girl, at the peak of her perfection as a golfer.

As with many other ideas which have come recently to the front, now that we know more about the brace, we find traces of it going way back into history! One of the finest pictures I have ever seen of a golfer standing to the ball was one of Mac Smith reproduced in the *American Golfer* some years ago, to my mind a perfect illustration of the correct set. I have it in my scrapbook and often take a peep at it, for we cannot refresh our memories too often. Study the photograph of Aubrey addressing the ball (page 74). Note especially the close relationship between this *set* and the actual hitting position; there is almost no difference between them, and that is why the good golfer *can feel his drive in his address.*

When you are learning golf it is most helpful to watch good golfers and to see how they apply the doctrines which your teacher has impressed upon you. Some years ago I took a pupil of mine to study the players at Sandwich. "They look so *firm*," was his comment. They looked firm because they started braced and retained the braced feeling right through the swing.

There is one other aspect of the brace that we must consider, that concerned with the position of the head.

Preparatory to the Swing

If the head and chin are turned slightly to the right (so that the ball is seen "out of the corner of the left eye," as one of my pupils put it), it will help the feel of the correct brace—mainly because it helps us to fix our shoulders, or rather helps our shoulders to resist the movement of the hips which is trying to pull the right shoulder forward (as it does pull forward the right knee, which does not resist).

I do not mind whether you say that this position of the head fixed the shoulders or merely that it helps to fix them, but I know that it is infinitely easier to brace correctly with the head slightly side-on in this way than when looking straight down. Also, as it brings the head and chin slightly *behind* the ball, it gives the right feeling that we are looking at the back of the ball.

For those who like delving into past theories and histories of the game, the following is illuminating. It is a translation from a book called *Le Jeu de Mail* which I picked up in Paris for 10 francs. It was written nearly two hundred years ago. The extract is from the chapter on "Attitude of the Body."

"The body should not be too straight nor too curved, but slightly bent" (note the nuance "curved" and "bent." Even a couple of centuries ago they had to be careful in picking their words!) "in order that in hitting, it shall be held up by the strength of the hips (*reins*) while turning slowly backwards from the waist, without losing the ball from view."

On Learning Golf

It is this half turn of the body that we call playing with the waist (or better, pivoting) which gives a wide circle to the club head.

The old book continues: "We should not lift the club too quickly but in order to (*uniquement*) and without allowing oneself to be carried away" (sway, we should say now), "wait a little (*se tenir un instant*) at the top of the swing (*la plus haute portée*) in order to hit through the plane"(amusing this, *sur le champ*) "with vigour, adding however, the force of the wrist (*la force du poignet*) without changing the position of the body, legs, or arms, in order to conserve the same union of adjustments which we have taken up at the address."

CHAPTER IX

Interlude for Instruction

o

WHAT WE MEAN WHEN WE SAY—

WHEN my boys at St. Cloud found a particularly annoying pupil, they usually managed on one pretext or another to pass him on to the Boss! So when one day I was told that Old Zambuck insisted upon having a personal lesson from myself, I suspected trouble ahead! However it turned out to be an entertaining and thought-provoking experience.

Of course he had not been christened Old Zambuck—except by my boys! He was a retired Advocate; in his time he had been a good sportsman and a successful second-class tennis player. Now he was mad about golf and spent a lot of time at it, though up to the day of which I write he had never been a direct pupil of mine.

On our way to the sheds he informed me that he would have come to me before but for the fact that he understood that I had certain fixed ideas and considered myself "something of an impressionist."

I gasped at that! Impressionism in golf was a new one on me. I certainly have studied deeply many impressionist pictures, without understanding a thing about them, and if I have the same effect on my pupils

On Learning Golf

as the pictures have on me—well, may heaven help my pupils!

"Now who told you I considered myself an impressionist?" I asked.

"Oh, Mr. So-and-So. You told him you tried to give a mind impression of how a shot was played, that the pupil had to translate into *feel*."

"Well I suppose that if trying to make you see in your mind how a movement works or what it feels like is impressionism—then I'm guilty! But I had never thought of it that way."

"I'm glad to hear it. I thought it was an attitude you assumed to impress people—knowing what snobs they are about such things."

"Oh you did!—Well, get that right out of your (silly old) head," said I somewhat piqued.

"Now don't get angry," he said. "Flaring up over nothing is another of your reputations!"

I said that he seemed to have gone around the village raking out my skeletons—and suggested that as it was a golf lesson, we might stick to the subject.

"Right," he answered. "Then how would you describe a teacher who told his pupils not to trouble about looking at the ball?"

I knew at once what he was driving at. "Well," I said, "if it were not I who had said that, I should say the teacher was a damned fool."

"But you *did* say it, to Mr. So-and-So!" he claimed in triumph.

What we Mean When we Say

"Of course I did, but as an individual prescription for an individual and very unusual case. He had got his eyes so glued to the ball, he was staring at it so rigidly, that he simply could not relax. In order to relax him I told him not to look at the ball."

"Did it work?"

"It did—very well, because the expression I used gave him the right impression of how he should view the ball."

"Ah, I see. You think that different pupils need different phrases to give them the same impression—and you use 'look at the ball,' 'peep at the ball,' or 'stare at the ball' accordingly?"

"Certainly. The difficulty in teaching golf is that what we have to teach is a correct *feel*, and neither demonstration nor words can do that directly. Sometimes it is almost a chance word or movement that gives the pupil the right impression—and then he picks up the *feel* in a flash."

"You must need a pretty good vocabulary for that," he suggested.

"Good in the sense of accurate, yes. But not necessarily extensive. You need a variety of words conveying more or less the same idea. And there are difficulties with lessons which, like this one, I give in French. For thirty years I have tried, and failed, to find the French equivalent for the English word 'swing'—and there isn't one!"

"By Jove, that is curious, but you are right."

On Learning Golf

"I know I am! But what can I do without the word 'swing'? The opposite of swing (in golf) is scoop. But no one will get the right idea of a sweeping swing by being told not to scoop!"

"Now I am enjoying this," said my pupil, warming to it. "So let us clear up some other 'teachers' phrases' that I may not have the right idea of. For instance, what about 'resist'?"

"As a matter of fact," said I, "I use the word 'resist' as little as possible. I prefer 'oppose.'"

"You do? And why?"

"Because 'resist' gives the impression that you *stop* the left side—for instance—in order to resist the blow. 'Oppose' suggests *opposition during movement* which is the correct conception."

"So! You mean that we must not feel the left side stop as we set our resistance on our way through the ball?"

"Certainly, most certainly, we must not. If you feel that it fixes your resistance on a certain spot, but if you feel you *oppose* the weight of the club head you can *oppose* it all the way up, down, and through—which is what you should do."

"But do you mean I must oppose the club head on the up swing?"

"Yes, if you will think of 'opposing' as 'force in the opposite direction'—which is the way to think of it. It is that and that alone which keeps the controlled swing *taut* and controlled."

What we Mean When we Say

"Good, so far! Now to the next. I have some difficulty in comprehending the word 'wait,' when you tell us to wait for the club head."

"Well 'wait' gives a fairly good impression if you take it simply in relation to the left heel. When you are told to 'wait for the club head' you are meant to delay your sweep through until your left heel has come well back to the ground. So the phrase is not well chosen. And also I do prefer the word 'delay' because 'wait' somewhat suggests stopping the whole swing—which is entirely the wrong idea. Stopping the whole swing is just as bad as not waiting at all—because in each case you will 'come down altogether.'"

"Which is wrong?"

"Certainly. The idea is to *start up all movements together but to come down one after the other*. The club head must follow the body down. If you 'wait' *for the club head to complete the up swing*, it will catch the body up and you will come down altogether."

"Let me ponder over that a bit. Now that is quite true and interesting to me because I used to wait all over, as you say, and however long I waited it never got me over the mistake it was supposed to correct, 'coming down *altogether*'—and in consequence *outside*. You have made me see why. If I delay the club head—not my whole swing—I shall feel the club head coming in *after*."

"I am very pleased with your deduction, which shows that you have absolutely grasped the idea. But

On Learning Golf

just another word about resist and oppose. Arising out of a pretty *jeu de mots* with which some pupils tried to trip me one evening—I evolved the following:

> When I resist I will become tight,
> When I oppose I will become taut.

—and from that anyone who has any sense of finesse with words can see how we poor golf Pros can go all sideways in our teaching! We must be neither tight nor slack at golf—we must be taut."

"Good! That is clear. Now there is another question I want to ask you. What is this 'lateral movement'?"

"So far as I know, it is a movement set up by the hips which allows the right hip to go to the right as we swing up and the left to the left as we go through. According to theory the closer the movement is kept to the line of flight, the less pernicious it is likely to be."

"The less pernicious? You do not like lateral movement?"

"I am totally opposed to it. How it arises you will see from the chapter on Golf Bogey No. 1 in my book."

"But I have not got your book."

"Well, hurry up and get it!"

"I will—but one more point first. Must I keep my wrists down as I address the ball?"

"You must not. If you do, the toe of your club will be off the ground. Also it is better to keep your wrists *up* with more or less a straight line through your arms,

What we Mean When we Say

wrists, and shafts, so that you can keep the *club head down* on the way back—which is different!"

"Must I always feel that I keep the club head down?"

"You bet you must! Use whichever phrase you like—'keep the club head down' or 'don't lift the club head.' They are positive and negative of the same idea."

"Now before we leave the question of wrists. Do I have to 'cock my wrists' on the back swing?"

"No, you do not! The wrists cock themselves. If you hold your wrists free to respond to the movement of the swing and to the momentum of the club head set up by that movement, the weight of the club head itself will be sufficient to cock the wrists for you."

"Then my wrists should be cocked! So why did you say they should not?"

"I did not say they should not be cocked, I said you do not cock them, which is quite different. You do wrongly when you grab hold of the club and actively *lift* the club head back over your shoulder. We do not lift the club head up—we swing it back and it goes up. Only when you can carry your club head back from the ball, will you be able to break your wrists on the way down."

"On the way down! Surely you mean at the top of the swing," he protested.

"Well," I said, "'At the top' will do for anyone but the topnotcher; so as you don't aspire that high you can keep it! But do remember anyway *not* to lift the

On Learning Golf

club head up with your hands, *or* to cock your wrists *actively.*"

"Then again—must I keep my left arm straight as I go up?"

"Certainly. But there again if you feel *wide* as you go up, as you should, your arm *will* be straight. Make the straightness an effect rather than a cause."

"Is the idea of keeping it straight to be able to pull down with the left arm from the top?"

"Oh dear no, no! Your left arm is straight to give you a wide swing so that your club head will come in from behind the ball, not from above it. But you do not pull down with your arms, you pull down from the legs and left side. If you start the swing down by grounding your left heel the rest of the body, shoulders, and arms, being reactive, will respond to this pull from the leg, and your arms and hands will be started down slowly and quietly—to gather speed as they get down behind the back of the ball."

"I congratulate you, Professor. That is a most eloquent and excellent explanation of how not to scoop—and in French too! Now, finally, what is back-spin? And is it the *only* way of stopping a ball from running over a green when it pitches on it, giving it a spin like the screw-back shot at billiards?"

"That is a fair comparison of golf back-spin. But what you people do not understand is the *amount* of back-spin to put on a ball in various conditions."

What we Mean When we Say

"Do you mean I can vary the amount of back-spin I impart? That must be terribly difficult."

"Exactly. It is, if you try yourself to put the back-spin on. Personally, I practically never try to put back-spin on the ball; *I leave it to the club to do so.*"

"But I love to see the ball pitch on the green, jump one bound forward, and then pull up dead—or even run back."

"So do I," said I. "But such shots are usually played out of a near bunker and the sand on the face of the club has something to do with them—as well as the fact that the soft sand has allowed us to get well under the ball. You can't play shots like that so well off a hard road!"

"But if you say I should not try to put back-spin on the ball, how can I stop it on the green?"

"Ah . . . There must *be* back-spin, but it must be only what is put on by the loft of the club."

I continued, "Did it ever occur to you that the degree of 'run' is practically independent of anything *you* may do? Try and get 'run' on a ball struck properly with a No. 8 iron. You can't do it. So do not bother about back-spin—leave that to your club, and the experts! Rely on accurate hitting, and then the fact that you have a lofted club will give you what you want."

"Why will it?"

"Because you have taken the ball below its center to give it height, you have automatically given it a cer-

On Learning Golf

tain amount of back-spin as well. You then have a combination of height and back-spin to stop the ball. The ball drops almost vertically out of the sky and would not run much even if it had no back-spin."

"You mean I ought to aim not at pure back-spin but at a kind of 'drop-shot' to stop the ball?"

"Exactly. It is the difference between throwing a ball overhand onto the green and tossing it on with an underhand lob. It is really a lob shot you want to develop. And let me tell you that the short shot played with a delicate lob is the most effective scoring shot in golf."

"Well I thank you, Professor—for a most illuminating half-hour. Good-day to you!"

And so we parted, each of us having learned something.

CHAPTER X

Centered on Wrist Action

THERE is no action in golf less understood than the use of the wrists, for curiously enough we do not have to work them, but we have to let them work themselves —like the hinges on a door.

This is important because the wrists will only be used correctly when we have the right idea of their correct mechanical action. If we get the wrong idea, the opening of the wrists in the region of the ball is bound to be mistimed. You will never get perfect timing if you try to flick the club head through the ball by wrist and hand action—perfect timing will come only when the opening of the wrists is brought about automatically by the momentum of the whole swing.

To put it in another way, the movements of the feet, legs and hips belong to the active, intentioned part of the down swing; the opening of the wrists belongs to the passive, purely reactive part of it. So keep at the forefront of your mind that the hands and wrists do not and must not "nip the club head through the ball."

The trouble in learning to let your wrists open themselves (which is what they must do) is, that at the top of the swing, the club head seems so far from the ball that you feel that, if you do not *help it down* with wrist

On Learning Golf

and hand action, it will never get there—or will get there so late as to make a horrible slice. The result is that you *do* work your wrists, you come down too soon, and *pull* instead of slicing! Low ground shots to the left are most frequently due to this premature and faulty wrist action.

Now this feel of the club head being a long way from the ball and a long way from your left side is actually a most desirable one. Register it in your *feel* cabinet, and if you can *widen* the gap between the club head and your left side, do so; you can never get it too wide. The gap means that you are "coming down one after another."

Personally I detest the word "flick." Apart from being an anæmic conception anyway, it suggests a *local* effort where there should be none. That is why teachers now prefer the word "flail" to describe the function of the wrists. You know the flail with which the peasant threshes his corn—two sticks connected by a free link—and you know he could not apply the same power anything like so effectively with a single solid stick. Well, your wrists are the link of the flail, the club the threshing stick.

Another image that has helped some of my pupils to visualize the development of a correct swing is that (in this section of the swing) our arms and the club form a *fan*—the line of the left arm being one edge of the fan, the club being the other. The two are pivoted together by the wrists and (like the two edges of an

Centered on Wrist Action

actual fan) may be shut close together *or* opened out at quite a wide angle. We open the fan partially on the up swing, complete the opening at the beginning of the down swing—and snap together again some two feet or more past the ball.

The hands and wrists are passive agents, they are not free agents—they do not decide in which direction they shall go; they go in the arc set out for them by the turning of the pivot. This is true of the up swing as well as the down. The pivot not only provides the power, it also controls direction—guiding the club head in its correct plane through the ball. That is why a good pivot is so important.

But we must not forget that we are going to learn golf by *feel;* so here is a little exercise that will teach you to detect and ever afterwards to recognize the difference between *feet activity* and *hand activity* at the beginning of the back swing.

Take up your normal stance before the ball. Then without movement of feet, pivot, shoulders, or arms, take the club head back a full three feet entirely by wrist and hand movement. Note the *feel.* Then re-address the ball (being careful this time to keep your left arm and the club shaft in a straight line from shoulder to club head). Now turn your body around *from the knees only* until your club head is a yard back again—making no use of any movement above the hips. Note the entirely different feel.

In the first case, your hands *lifted* the club head

On Learning Golf

back; in the second, your pivot *carried* it back, and you will have felt at once that the latter is much the smoother and much the more consistent way. It is this carry back beginning at the pivot which I want you to cultivate.

Please do not think that I am making an undue fuss about a trifle in going to such lengths to introduce you to the right *feel* at the beginning of the swing. I will go so far as to say that your progress will be very largely decided by whether or not you get this back swing right—once you get the correct feel of the carry back, you will find the rest of the swing *flowing from it* naturally. So, do study this feel quite profoundly. Properly considered it is the whole golf feel, because this initial carry back is the whole swing in embryo.

But now let us carry our experiment in feel a further stage. Do it mentally this time. Go (in your mind) to the top of your swing and then get the feeling of starting the down swing by the two different methods by which you started the carry back. That is, the first time feel that you start the down swing with hand and wrist movement only, the second time feel that you start it *from the knees.*

Now if you were observant of feel in your first experiment (the carry back), this second one will give you quite a vivid idea of what the beginning of the down movement should feel like. Of course it is the movement starting from the knees that is correct; it enables you to come down without using the hands

Centered on Wrist Action

actively. You will feel your hands, arms, and wrists coming down *broken back*—the wrists beginning to drop down towards the ball. This is what we mean by "dropping the wrists from the top" and "passive hand work."

So at each of the points we have examined there are two feels—the activity from the knees and the passivity of hands and wrists. The most notable difference is that at point 1 the wrists are straight while at point 2 they are broken. How they break on the up swing is our next study.

This introduces the question of *tension*, how tightly we hold our club and consequently our wrists—for if we grip the club with a stranglehold, our wrists will become inflexible. We want them and indeed our whole body flexible; so our grip should be light and sensitive.

As we take the club head back, from the knees, though the wrists have not taken part in the carry back, they will have been *tightened*—to hold the club shaft in a straight line with the left arm. *How much* should we tighten here? Just as little as will serve to carry away the club head where it should go; any more and you lose flexibility.

Those of us who have been in the Navy know what it means to "take up the slack"—"take the strain"—"haul away." They are three degrees of tension. Well, in golf we must always take up the slack, but we are never at haul tension until close behind the ball. Mostly we

On Learning Golf

must use just enough tension to take the strain—to feel taut without feeling *tight*.

Now, having taken up the strain put on our wrists by the carry back from the pivot, we find that as the club head begins to gather speed and momentum on the way back and up, the strain on the wrists lessens (so our tension on them can lessen) and towards the top of the swing they again become perfectly free from all strain. The tension we noticed on the way back was forced on us by the weight of the club—and the earlier we can get rid of this on the way up the better for our swing. And the tension will certainly decrease as experience teaches us how very little of it is needed, as we become familiar with the *feel* of a good swing. A good slow waggle will take a surprising amount of tension off our uptake.

Next, *when* do the wrists break, when should they break? This is an important point, and I did not make up my mind about it until I had made a close study of it in the swings of Lady Amory (Miss Wethered), Harry Vardon, Bobby Jones, and Henry Cotton. My conclusion is that the wrists should break as *late* as possible.

In order to break the wrists as late as possible on the back swing, we must carry our hands back quite a long way—indeed as far as possible, before we break. "It feels like an eternity!" a pupil once remarked to me. Well it does if you have always done the opposite:

Centered on Wrist Action

that is broken your wrists as the initial movement of the carry back. *Now* you feel your wrists will never break as you go up—and as a matter of fact that is a true feeling, because they actually only break when you are beginning to feel you are on the way down (see the note on the top of the swing on page 28).

Now let me describe an important little local movement hidden in this part of the swing—the *reverse*. The reverse is the part of the swing in which the club head is thrown over and pulled down. It requires a special name because it has a special *feel*, a feel curiously detached from that of the rest of the swing. We have our main feel of control and power down in our nether regions, but at the moment of reverse we are conscious of something happening up above, which is not in accordance with what we are doing down below.

What happens at the reverse is that the club head—having so far to go—takes longer to get to the end of its journey back than does the body, the turn of which is soon exhausted. So before the club head has arrived, the body has begun to come back. As to check the return body movement, *or* to check the completion of the club head's travel, would create an undesirable pause in the flow, we let them go on, and the club finds itself *behind* the body movement both *in time* and *in position*. This is as it should be.

When we are told to allow our wrists free play at the summit of the swing, it is so that we shall not break

On Learning Golf

up—by introducing muscular hand force—the flow of movement which we have intentionally set up in the reverse region.

The *feel* in this region is that the club head is still going back when our force center begins to pull forward. The wrists do not break at a given point; their break is a retarded action *set up to delay the club head* and yet to keep the movement smooth. The swing is a continuous flow of movement, and we destroy its continuous character if we divide it arbitrarily into two parts—"up swing" and "down swing." There is no up swing and no down swing; there is *the swing* complete. For the first three feet back from the ball we are "all together," but after that the club head—owing to the longer path it must take—loses ground, which it only catches up at the moment of impact with the ball. It *will* catch up then, even if you try to prevent it, and the further it has lagged behind, the faster it must travel to catch up.

So far in this chapter we have been concerned in analyzing the *local feels* which occur in the course of the swing, but this is only because, like the musician, the golfer has to de-compose a piece before he can play it. But the *feel* at golf is a transitory one, and soon these transitory local feels blend into the feel of the swing as a whole.

The fluency of the swing becomes greater as the swing gathers speed, and when the ball is swept from the tee, the flick of the wrists (hateful expression) has

Centered on Wrist Action

become a violent sweep—*violent* because of it's force, a *sweep* because of its fluency.

We are told and have evidence in the "flickers" that the wrists open as we come into contact with the ball, but this opening is not something that the wrists *do*, but something which they cannot help happening. And the art lies not in making the wrists open but in postponing their opening as late as possible.

As the club head arrives in the region of the ball, our body (because of its comparatively short degree of action) has already got back into its "opposing" position, with left heel back on the turf, left side straight and firm, and right hip twisted into the left one—the whole giving a sense of secure *brace* to the whole body. By this time the arms are already half-way down, but the wrists are still pulled back. But now owing to the forward pull of the hips and the gathering momentum of the club head, something must happen—and what happens is that we can no longer keep the club head from flying past the ball.

We have done everything possible to delay the club head and to inhibit wrist movement, but finally the club head gets out of control (this is literally true) and flashes through the ball as if mad with rage!

Now this is as it should be. We purposely set up a state that would leave the club head free and unchecked in this region of the swing, and we must see to it that we do not interfere in any way with its ferocious passage through the ball. There will almost inevitably

On Learning Golf

be some tendency to rigidity due to local necessities in this region (as in the initial take-up), but we must not feel the slightest check or guide attempting to control the club head. *Let its furious assault die away into a perfect follow through.*

Do not hold or check or guide the club head but keep the left side firm and rigid and play on around it. That is the only way of keeping the fury of the club head on the right path. You have unleashed a storm, and all you can do is to control the center from which came its force *and from which it will die away.* Feel centered and balanced.

If after reading the foregoing you come to the conclusion that the best thing to do with your wrists is nothing at all, my exposition has been successful. Since probably no one has told you before that your wrists *are only a link,* you cannot be blamed for not having realized it!

Too many people try to do something with their hands, thinking this to be *wrist action.* But when you analyze it, there is no deliberately induced action in the golf swing which corresponds to the mythical "flick of the wrists." Anyway, the word flick is appropriate when we speak of removing ash from a cigarette—but utterly out of place in a movement which sweeps a golf ball two hundred and fifty yards down the fairway.

If you have built up a good powerful central organization around which you whirl your club, the more

Centered on Wrist Action

you leave your wrists to their own sphere of activity the better will be your stroking. And the proper sphere of activity of your wrists is to act as the link in the flail with which you sweep the ball away.

Recently I was explaining to a coming champion my deduction that hand work wrongly applied to flick the club head through the ball was the commonest misconception in golf. He thought this over, and then said that he had read (and now began to understand what Bobby Jones meant when he wrote it) that on his way through the ball Bobby Jones felt that he was "free-wheeling."

The American mind is inventive of and receptive to the vivid modern expression, and Bobby Jones coined a great one in "free-wheeling" through the ball—as a corrective to the general misconception of the flick of the wrists being a sharp hand and arm attack applied directly to the ball.

THE GRIP

POINTS TO STUDY

Only two knuckles of the left hand are showing.

The right hand is held well on top of the shaft. The first finger of the right hand is held as on a "trigger" shooting down at the ball—it will be pushing against the back of the shaft. It is pinched into its position by the thumb.

The right elbow is held down, and in consequence the right wrist is arched upward.

The hands are close together, so the two wrists are close together and can operate as one large hinge.

The elbows are *braced*. They seem to be held close to the body, but are in fact held close together by the brace.

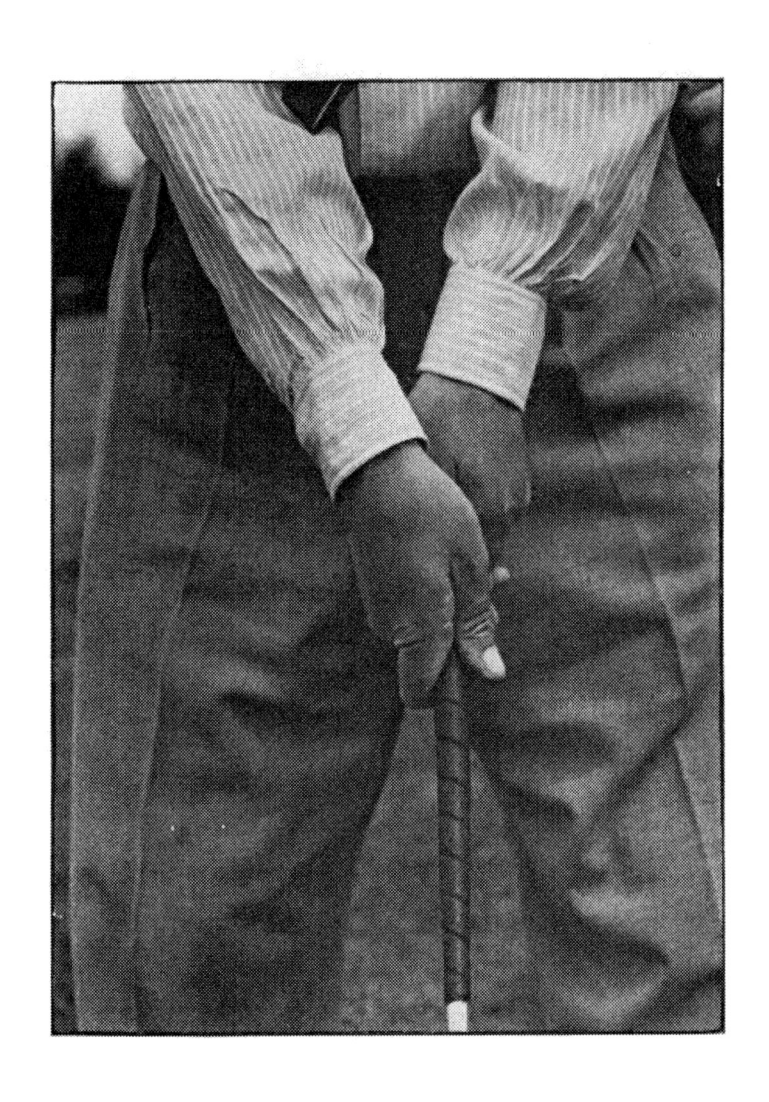

THE GRIP

PERCY

CHAPTER XI

To Keep (or not to keep) Your Eye on the Ball

○

I SUPPOSE the most often repeated piece of advice in the whole realm of golf is "keep your eye on the ball." It is given and accepted as a profound golfing truth (which properly understood it is), but it is necessary to examine what we mean by it and how it fits into the rest of our golfing program.

Very early in my teaching of a new pupil I tell him to keep his eye on the ball, because I know that unless he does so he will never achieve any class as a golfer. But I do not harp on the idea or rub it in—I point out that its importance actually lies less in the sight of the ball than in the *reactions* which it produces —for instance that it keeps our heads still.

And I put this emphasis on the *reactions* rather than on the sight of the ball because, to my mind, it is only the bad golfer who actually sees the ball out of his eyes. The good golfer I am convinced *feels* where the ball is more than *sees* it.

Now to the ordinary golfer that may seem an absurd statement, or if he does accept it, it may be confusing. So I will try to clarify my meaning.

On Learning Golf

When Aubrey and I were playing a lot together, we were often congratulated upon the *deftness* of our short game—and the congratulations were usually followed by the comment, "How long you keep your head down after the ball has gone!" Their idea was obviously that I kept my head down because it enabled me to "keep my eye on the ball." But what I was really doing was to keep my head down in order to retain the *feel* of the swing and to keep my controls going even though the ball had been dispatched. Few of the spectators realized that I often *played these shots with my eyes shut;* yet I did so.

But when I play with my eyes shut, my *senses are wide open*. My main concern was to see that my general muscular feel and sense of balance went right through to the end. Not until the follow-through was finished did I look up to see where the ball had gone. I never miss a shot through looking up too quickly; I do sometimes miss one through fear of missing it! The primary fault is not in looking up but in *losing the feel of the swing*.

Incidentally I have taught many pupils to play beautiful pitch shots without looking at the ball. One very well-known golfer to whom I taught this brought out his "better-half" to watch him "do his circus stuff." He played some beautiful shots high in the air over gaping bunkers, dropping close around the pin every time and all the while looking me straight in the face. His wife was utterly astonished; then she saw the funny

To Keep Your Eye on the Ball

side of it and laughed herself nearly into hysterics!

My view is that the good golfer can only *see* the ball when his swing is working smoothly, and then it looks as big as a tennis ball! The beginner *sees* the ball in another way, and because of this, more often than not he misses it. His attention is so concentrated upon seeing the ball that he cannot feel his swing operate. The business of seeing the ball occupies him too exclusively.

Do I mean by that that the beginner needs to *learn* how to see the ball? That is exactly what I do mean. He must learn *not* to see the ball to the exclusion of all his other senses. So when I tell a pupil to keep his eye on the ball I *at once* go on to the work of building up *a swing that makes looking at the ball a necessity*. Of course *every* pupil "looks up" badly at first to have the pleasure of seeing where the ball has gone, but this is a primitive stage and soon over.

In the next stage, when I am impressing him more and more with swinging correctly, I find that he often becomes so engrossed in the swing as to be unable to remember to keep his eye on the ball. But in such a case I believe the cure must come by making the "head down" a natural outcome of the swing. If I simply insist upon "head down," I run a risk of getting my pupil all stiffened up, "frozen on the ball" as we call it, and consequently only able to make hacking, chopping movements.

Now in this matter of seeing the ball, I would ask

On Learning Golf

you to consider a golfer at the other end of the scale. How does a very good golfer *see* the ball? In my opinion, through his very highly developed sense of feel, he sees the ball (in some proportion) through his hands.

Sees through his hands? Perhaps the idea is not so fanciful as it might seem. I began to think about it first after I had read an article by Sir Herbert Barker some years ago. This is what he said: "We take our hands too much for granted. Their possibilities and powers are seldom discovered or developed. Most people pass through life with these two implements untrained, unexplored, unknown. . . ." Then he goes on: "When we take for granted the localization of our senses in certain organs we go too fast. Localized they are, but not completely so." Then at a later date my interest was reawakened by the declaration of Dr. Fougools, the French savant, that in the skins of our hands are potential eyes. He says that they are nerve eyes atrophied for the simple reason that we have developed two ocular instruments so much superior to them.

Now to my mind the value of that idea to the golfer lies largely in an idea which it promotes, that perhaps the greatest value of "keeping your eye on the ball" is the assistance which it gives in building up *sight through feel*.

For whatever may be the eventual verdict of science upon the tentatively advanced hypothesis of the two famous men quoted above, I can assure you that some

To Keep Your Eye on the Ball

sort of sight through feel is certainly possible. I have developed it myself, as have many other first-class golfers. I can *see* the face of the club and the angle it is at the top of my swing (when it is "out of sight" behind the back of my head), and long before I lift my head, I can *see* the ball fly away with the exact curve which I know my shot has given it.

But let us leave these metaphysical regions and come back to the ordinary golfer. Why is it that so often he can make perfect swings when the ball is *not* there, yet he becomes semi-petrified and makes the most ridiculous shots as soon as there *is* a ball, even a ball carefully perched on a perfectly prepared tee, for him to hit? And what would happen if you could put down an invisible ball for him? Is it knowing that the ball is there that upsets his swing or is it the *sight* of it?

Anyway the invisible ball reminds me of a story! A threesome had just driven off the first tee when a stranger to the players asked if he might join in. "Why certainly, with pleasure," they said. The stranger stuck his wooden tee in the turf, made a beautiful swing at an imaginary ball on it, and went half-way down the fairway and "played" his second similarly with an iron. His second "pitched" on the green, and he carefully went through the motions of taking one putt for a three!

Not unnaturally, his fellow-players asked him what was the idea of dispensing with the ball. He explained it simply enough. *With* a ball, he said, he never got

On Learning Golf

around in less than 110, but *without* it he could rely upon being somewhere in the low 70's.

The next day he brought a friend along, and the threesome followed as a gallery. On the first green an argument arose, and the gallery came up to find out what was causing the trouble. Their companion of the previous day smiled at them and explained. "You see," he said, "I have laid him a stymie *and he does not know the rules!*"

A charming story, don't you think?

If you think this too fanciful (though the tale is true), it was recalled to my mind by a very practical job which I have recently undertaken—the re-education of a golfer who had not played *except in his imagination* for fifteen years. He was married at about that time and one of his marriage vows was not to play golf at week-ends. He had little other time to play, so when now and again he was able to get away in the week he would lunch at the club and then play nine holes *with an imaginary ball.* Something happened to the union, and he is now playing again. And I assure you that, with two or three lessons after his fifteen-year break, he was as good as ever he had been, and now, after a dozen or so, he is quite a few strokes better than he was when he renounced playing.

But we must come back (again!) to the ordinary golfer who finds that the ball has a devastating effect on his swing. Why is this so?

It is so because the ordinary golfer is an unrepentant

To Keep Your Eye on the Ball

end-gainer. When he sees the ball, he becomes obsessed with the idea of hitting it; the ball is made the *climax* or the *end* of his activity. That is to say, the highest speed attained by his club head is at the moment of impact, or, much worse still, he may try to stop the club head as soon as it has struck the ball. That is the effect of seeing the ball as something to be hit.

Now we know that for maximum effectiveness the highest speed attained by our club head (the dynamic center of our swing) must be some way past the ball—two feet past at least. So in one sense you must simply ignore the point in your swing where the ball sits on the tee. You must swing past it exactly as if it were not there. You must not get your eye frozen onto the ball, nor must you get your mind concerned with the problem of how far, how high, and how straight you are going to hit it.

The point I am making is that it is possible for us to be too conscious of the ball, for the ball to have too much of our attention. I suggested this to a pupil one day, and he retorted that in that case I should not give him a shining white ball to play with—a green or pink one would be less insistent. As a matter of fact he had some balls painted various colors and experimented with them with quite interesting results. But I had to point out that he was on the wrong track anyway. We use a white ball exactly because it *is* the easiest to see—and it is the *degree of attention* that is neces-

On Learning Golf

sary to enable us to keep the eye on the ball that is the critical point.

Let me put it this way:

(*a*) You must not make an undue effort to keep your eye on the ball,

but

(*b*) You must just keep your eye on the ball.

Here you see my difficulty again—the difficulty of finding a phrase that will accurately express a subtle shade of feeling. And however I express it, every reader will read and visualize it differently.

I remember one lady who came to me with her swing terribly constricted and tied up by *looking too intently at the ball*. She had no great physique, but she had patience and an analytical mind, and we soon had her sweeping the ball away in good style.

Knowing her to be an intelligent woman capable of expressing herself, and an interesting amateur painter, I asked her if she could explain the difference in her attitude to the ball since we had "united" her swing —and whether she saw it differently now. Her reply was worth pondering over.

"I cannot explain why," she said, "but now I never think of the ball. I am busy trying to feel how I should swing the club. Really I do not think I can tell you if I actually *see* the ball at all now . . . yes I do, but not in the old way. It used to look like craters in the moon, now it looks like a star in the Milky Way."

To Keep Your Eye on the Ball

Seeing my look of surprise she explained, "It used to be a huge, frightening, gray object, pitted with cavities; now it is a little star somewhere in the path of my wide sweeping swing."

Now that lady had found the joy of golf through getting an altered conception of the ball. For the joy of golf is to feel the ball snugly gathered up and thrown off the face of the club. In a sense no one can teach you that, you must find it for yourself—but some of us can certainly help you to find it, by giving you an understanding of what you are seeking.

The golf swing is governed by a chain of controls, and when the ball is introduced, it must not destroy, weaken, or dislocate any of them. Let us take four of the principal controls, purposely taken from points widely apart in the swing so as to represent the whole movement. Here they are:

1. Pivot.
2. Bring down the left heel early in the down swing.
3. Allow the wrists to break back slowly.
4. Continue the stroke on, through and around the left side.

These are just a selection of possible controls. They can be replaced by others or added to. But if a player will learn them thoroughly, by doing them slowly one after the other until they are *linked up* in his mind and muscles, he will become at least a decent golfer.

But if having got him this far, when he misses a shot I suddenly say to him, "You looked up!" the chances

On Learning Golf

are that he will then look at the ball so intently, with such fixed purpose, that he will miss the next shot too! What he has to do to get things right is to try not to look up but without interfering with his basic controls. In fact, the "not looking up" must become a new link in the chain of controls. You do *not* weaken a chain by adding more links to it unless the new links are weak.

As I see it, good teaching must be based upon giving the pupil a few fundamental controls that will never need to be altered but that can be added to, packed round, and supported by other controls as the pupil's game develops. But the essentials are that the early controls shall never need to be altered and that other controls which are added later must fit in with them; *never contradict them.* I can assure you that one needs a very sound knowledge of golf (and an extensive one of human capacities and make-up) to teach that way.

Further, when something goes wrong and a pupil loses his game, it will not do to say what is wrong and so to emphasize this wrong point that it attains undue importance in the pupil's mind. If you do that he will so concentrate upon getting that one point right that he will throw everything else *wrong.*

For instance a pupil comes along for a lesson because he has gone off his game badly. I see he is ducking his right shoulder and bending his knees and showing all sorts of faults which flow from these two. Now in my experience it is no use at all pointing out

To Keep Your Eye on the Ball

these faults to him. What I normally do, if I know him well enough, is to ask him what time he went to bed the previous night—and to suggest that he brace himself up a bit or he may fall to pieces—also that it is impossible to teach golf to a fellow who is practically down on his knees.

You would be surprised at the number of specific faults which I have cured that way! In fact it hardly ever fails. When your game goes to bits, *try bracing yourself up.*

Sometimes of course one *has* to be more specific, but even then I rarely point out the obvious fault *as* being an obvious fault.

Suppose a pupil comes to me and I see that his swing is too vertical; he is picking up his club head too quickly and so breaking his wrists (and even bending his left arm) too early. Plenty of faults to point out, but I do not point them out. What I do point out is that *he is losing width,* and in a short time just *keeping wide* will straighten his arm and correct the other faults. To get to this stage, I say to him every now and again, "That's fine, *keep wide*, don't stiffen, don't hurry, just keep wide." Soon he will begin to feel his swing again, and in a little it will be back to normal or maybe better than normal.

You may feel disposed to remind me that this chapter is supposed to be about keeping your eye on the ball! So it is, but these digressions on the controls have not cropped up by accident. I have introduced them

On Learning Golf

here to illustrate the point (which I keep making because it is so fundamentally important) that any *one* feature of the swing is of no use to a golfer and cannot even be understood unless it is linked up with all the other features. You can set a ball on your table and sit in a chair and learn to look at it all the evening, but that will teach you nothing at all about how to look at the ball in your swing. And as a golfer that is what you want to learn to do.

CHAPTER XII

Interlude for Instruction

IT IS THE PUPIL WHO MUST LEARN

THESE "Interludes for Instruction" will show you among other things why my job is so fascinating—at least to anyone like myself who is as interested in human beings as he is in golf. That dual interest I may tell you is an effective substitute for some of the qualities which I have *not* got: patience, for instance!

Pupils are continually telling me how much they admire my patience, but my family (who know me better) will tell you that I am one of the most impatient people imaginable with an almost objectionably insistent temperament. So when a pupil tells me I am very patient, I say, "You think so! But what you take for patience is simply the result of ripe experience. I am trying to build up good golfing habits in you, and I know that habits—good or bad, in golf or outside it—need time to consolidate."

Indeed, I remember one pupil of mine who brought a Professor of Philosophy along to survey my lesson. Having watched me for some time he said to my pupil, "He is creating instincts." I said nothing to that, but thought a lot! I had visualized my work as the creating of habits, but if he was right and it went back a further stage to the creation of instincts—then I would need

On Learning Golf

all the patience I could muster, if it was patience which enabled me to keep my good humor when a pupil misses the ball ten or twenty times in succession. Of course, I do not get out of patience when this happens. I simply say, "Carry on—don't worry, you will hit a good one soon." The point being that the pupil is doing as well as he can with the experience at his disposal. When he has had more experience, he will do better, but meanwhile neither my impatience nor his own will help him.

Now I want to describe a lesson which I once gave to a man and his wife. She was an Englishwoman and he a Japanese diplomat. The interesting point it illustrates is the completely different approach of two people, sympathetically akin, both wishing to learn to play a decent game of golf, yet completely opposite in inherent gifts and with absolutely different conceptions of the golf swing.

They were both playing enough *bad* golf shots to convince them that they were wrong somewhere; so they came to me for advice. Though both were temporary members of St. Cloud, I fortunately took them in my Indoor School—fortunately, because the big mirrors which I have before each driving net there happened to be the very thing necessary for one of them.

I gave each of them a couple of half-hour lessons. She was English and so should have understood me much better than he did. As a matter of fact he hardly understood a word I said and never answered more

It is the Pupil Who Must Learn

than an unconvinced and muttered, "Yes" or "No."

Yet look at this very odd sequel. After the lessons I did not see either of them for some weeks, except to wave them good-day on the course once or twice. Then she came back to the school alone to see me.

"Do you know," she said, "my husband has made remarkable progress since those two lessons, but I have not. In fact I am worse than ever. It beats me; you did nothing for my husband but tell him to keep his balance and not dip his shoulders—and even *that* you had to do by signs, yet hey presto!—he is a reformed golfer. And I, who had the full benefit of all your eloquence, am *worse* not better. I think I shall have to give the game up."

Then we came to it. Would I please tell her frankly if she was too fat (though I don't think she used that word) to ever play good golf. She could not resist a glance at me and a queried, "You are not *thin* for a golfer are you?"

I will not say that I felt flattered by the comparison, but anyway I told her to count the question of size *out*. A very highly placed pupil of mine told me once that the lightest partner he had ever danced with was a woman who weighed over two hundred pounds. I told her this, and, from the quizzical way she looked at me, I knew I had scored a point. So I went all out for game and set!

"May I be permitted to tell you what your real trouble is, Madam?" She nodded assent. "It is nothing

On Learning Golf

to do with your figure," I said. "It is that you cannot see, neither can you listen."

There was a slightly painful silence, which I waited for her to break—which she did by stammering that she did not understand.

"Don't you?" said I. "Well, I mean that, so far as learning goes, you are deaf and blind. Is *that* clear?"

"Yes," she said, "that is too brutal to be misunderstood. You might have put it in another way."

"Impossible," I said. "That is just the literal truth. You did not listen to what I told you *or* see what I demonstrated. Had you done so, you would not have got your game into its present mess.

"So far as your husband is concerned, he is deaf and dumb—so far as conversation with me is concerned—*but he is not blind*. He can see, and his eyes enabled him to pick out the essentials of my lesson."

"And what were they?"

"Well he had seen that all good golfers turn away from the ball, so he did so too. He did it wrongly because someone had told him to keep his eyes on the ball (probably *you* told him; it is an English idiom), and he dipped his shoulders in consequence. All he had to pick up from me was that to see the ball you need not dip the shoulders. He used his sense of sight and being naturally intelligent *got his pivot right*."

"But do you mean to suggest that he sees more or sees differently from the way *I* see?" she asked.

"Of course he does."

It is the Pupil Who Must Learn

"But being able to understand what you say should more than counterbalance that?"

"Maybe!" said I. "But don't forget that you have not only two chances of being right, you have also two chances of being wrong *and you took them both*! He got an extraordinarily pure conception of the movement by sight alone—and as he has probably more brains than the two of us put together, he seems to me to have all the advantages!"

"Well," she said quietly, "I think you may be right."

"Of course I am right. *Nothing* verbal can replace an intelligent visual conception of the swing. You have never seen a swing as your husband has seen it, because it is obvious from your own swing that you think the golfer's arms produce the power, like the arms of the windmill. This is not so; the golfer's powerhouse is below the waist. If he is a good golfer, he *never* hits with his arms. He gets his power by twist or *spin*."

I took up a wooden tee between thumb and first finger and *spun* it, like a top. "That is golf mechanics in its purest form," I said.

"But you don't expect a stout old lady like me to spin?"

"Why not! You do in the ballroom; why not on the golf course? And you need not worry about the slim flapper; she doesn't spin too well! *You* can turn on the pivot, and if you do, you will play good golf. But so long as you *slide* you are doomed."

"You suggest I slide?"

On Learning Golf

"Yes, you do," I said. "You don't turn because you are afraid of missing the ball. So you stand close to the ball and try to make up for the restriction which this puts on your power by *sliding* over the ball. It is a hopeless style.

"Your husband is a man and links cause and effect. He sees all good golfers play in a certain way; so he plays that way too. You, being a woman, do not care to consider causes, and the effect you want is to get someone to say, 'Good shot!' as your ball creeps off the tee. But you cannot earn the 'Good shot!' unless you concentrate on the *cause, on a good swing*.

"Now," I continued, "let me see you make a few swings first without a ball and then with one."

"Oh," she replied, "I can always swing well when there is no ball."

"Why?" I asked.

"That is what *I* want to know. Why *should* a stupid little ball perched up there ruin my swing?"

I chuckled. "Because you try to hit it!" I said.

"But surely I must try to hit it."

"Surely you must not! What you must try to do is to swing your club. Which at the moment means you must concentrate on pivoting *not* on hitting the ball."

"Don't you *try* to hit the ball?" she asked woman-like.

"No. I try to swing my club head correctly (that is, from my legs), so that it swings past the ball, taking the ball in its passage."

It is the Pupil Who Must Learn

"Then you said I was all wrong in what I did with my hands and arms. What should I do with them?"

"Just keep them out as *wide* as you can. You will feel you are stretching down when you near the ball, and that is good. What you must never feel is that you are lifting the club head, either on the way back or through. If you *lift*, you will *scoop* not *swing*."

"But how can I get my club head up over my shoulder if I do not lift it there with my arms?"

"Study and practice the pivot *and you will see!* Actually of course, the arms *do* lift the club, but it should not be an independent arm movement; it should be reactive—simply transmitting the power from the pivot. You say you cannot keep your left arm straight, and that is another certain sign that your idea of power is up and down with the arms, whereas ours is around and along from the pivot."

She picked up a club and took a few swings, much shorter than before, the body much more stretched and with more leg work.

"Is that more the idea?" she asked.

"Much more."

"But I am not hitting the ball any better!"

"Not yet, but you will, because you are now beginning to swing correctly."

"But I feel I can never connect with the ball from away back there."

"Oh yes, you will, very shortly too, and with much more consistency than with your old scoop."

On Learning Golf

"But even if I *do,* I feel I have no *power* at all that way. I cannot use my wrists."

"You mean you cannot use your hands and arms. That is exactly what we have been aiming at! Actually *using* the wrists in golf is a most delicate business, possible only to the very good player. When you think you are using your wrists, you are simply pulling the club down with your arms as fast as it will come."

"Well if *I don't* pull it down, how am I going to get it to go swiftly through the ball?"

"Curiously enough you get maximum club head speed at the ball by exactly the opposite of your 'pulling down' plan. You get it by *delaying* the club head so that it lags behind the rest of the swing and then rushes forward. To get this effect you must let your wrists be a *free link*—any attempt to use them in your stage of experience will simply kill the speed of the club head."

"And that 'delay the club head?' Is that what you mean when you say 'swing slowly'?"

"Yes. Curiously, again, the sweeping swing which gives you maximum club head speed does not *feel* fast."

"Well, I will try! But it all sounds so illogical, and I *do* like to know what I am doing and why."

"I am delighted to hear that, because it means you will make progress. But do not try too hard to understand with your mind. So you will begin to connect with the ball, and then new sensations, or feelings,

It is the Pupil Who Must Learn

will develop, and these will give you a new and much clearer conception of what is going on."

"So! And how do I set about it now?"

"Well, just stand in front of your ball, not curved over it but slightly bent down and out towards it. Then without moving sideways, turn first back and then forward *from the pivot*. Now look at the ball, but do not stare at it or bend to get a closer view! *Peep* at it, a sly look at the ball is better than a stare. Don't hold your club too tight, for, if you do, your wrists will become wooden and wooden wrists are useless. And try to hold your club with no more tension at the top of the swing than you use at the address. You must hold the club *firmly*, neither tightly nor loosely, but firmly."

"But that reminds me. Will my grip do?"

"For what you need now, yes. You must realize that what you do now is done *grosso modo*, is done in a general sense and is not necessarily exact in detail. As time goes on and you become more familiar with the working of the swing as a whole, we may modify the different sections."

"You mean that some day we will study the grip or the stance in detail?"

"Exactly. But not too soon. It is hopeless for a beginner to concentrate on some single point and work at it and struggle to get it right when what he should be doing is to get some sort of *movement* going, based upon the correct principles of swing—which are a good

On Learning Golf

pivot and a wide-sweeping movement, with good central balance and power from the feet and legs.

"All the working members of the golf swing are related and linked up, and it is the perfect co-ordination of movements that makes the good player. Experience has shown me that where most people go wrong when they take up golf is in imagining that the power must be produced by the hands and arms. Yet the fact that they put nails in their shoes should tell them where the power comes from!"

My pupil took a few more swings and swept one or two balls away quite nicely.

"I admit that they begin to go a bit better and to *feel* better. But it is sheer luck if they go straight!"

"Why luck?"

"Because when I swing as you tell me, I have no idea of where the hole is *or* where I am aiming the ball. I feel too far from the ball to be able to guide it down the middle."

"Good, because that is not the way to get it down the middle anyway. Listen; when you have learned to sweep the ball away more or less truly four or five or six times in succession, you will begin to *feel* a sense of direction. You will begin to feel that when you operate in a certain manner, your ball will go in a certain direction. The ball will keep this direction as long as you keep the feel of the swing, but if you pull the swing out of shape or try to constrict it by trying to *guide* the ball, all certainty of direction is lost."

It is the Pupil Who Must Learn

"Then I must definitely not try to drive the ball down the middle?"

"You definitely must not. You have tried to do that for years and have gradually become worse and worse. That is why you came to me for advice."

"Well you have given me plenty," she said somewhat ruefully.

"Yes," I replied. "It does sound very complicated all in a mass like that. It seems absurd to make such hard work of a game. But much of your trouble is in getting rid of false ideas and bad habits. Once you get on the right lines and begin to progress, like your husband, you will get a lot of fun out of working out each new problem as it arises. For each new sensation brings a new idea which must be fitted into your golfing system as a whole. That is the whole trick of progressing at golf: to add what you learn to what you already know."

When we parted she was doubtful if she ever *could* progress! But I am happy to say that she is now a very decent golfer, and an intelligent and analytic one.

CHAPTER XIII

The Feeling of In-to-Out

o

IT is now time for us boldly to approach a subject which we have already skirted round and touched the fringes of, the in-to-out theory about which so much has been heard in recent years. We have already considered certain aspects of it in the chapters on "Golf Bogey No. 1," and "Preparatory to the Swing." Now in this chapter I want to help you to feel how to swing from in-to-out, a thing of which many people realize the importance without being able to put it into practice.

Firstly what is this "in-to-out"? It is the feeling of swinging the club head *not* directly down the line of flight, but from *inside* this line as the ball is approached to *outside* the line in the follow through. *The feeling that this is the path taken by the club head is essential to a good swing. Therefore the fact that scientific analysis can prove that at the impact the club head does actually follow the line of flight exactly can be ignored. You play golf by feeling, not by scientific analysis.*

This feeling of in-to-out is intimately connected with that other feeling referred to in the chapter on

The Feeling of In-to-Out

"Preparatory to the Swing," that of being set inwards and *behind the ball*. The long straight drive that covers the pin all the way is the result of a swing which you *feel* travels from in-to-out. This is what we all refer to as an in-to-out swing; a shot in which the club head does actually take this path (as distinct from being felt to take it) is only played by the first-class golfer when he wants to put *pull* on the ball. And if you will think it out, that suggests why the in-to-out feeling is something that we teachers try to instill into every pupil.

The point being that, while an exaggerated in-to-out feel gives *pull*, the correct in-to-out feel gives straightness and *no* in-to-out feel (that is, the feeling that the club head goes along the line of flight) gives *slice*.

The advantage of the modern in-to-out swing is seen in both the flight and the run of the ball. Hit with the correct in-to-out feel, the ball is given the very minimum of backspin—consequently it "floats" through the air and, when it pitches, takes its natural spin forward, instead of kicking sideways as an undercut ball tends to do, as every lawn-tennis player knows.

To return to the subject of slice. The man who gave me my first job as a professional thirty-five years ago was the late H. L. Curtis—father of the present Pro at Queen's Park, Bournemouth. He told me many years later that he was doubtful about giving me the job, but having done so he started me off with a very

On Learning Golf

sound piece of advice. "Now laddie," he said, "if you ever want to make good at this business, you had better find out *how to teach people not to slice.*"

Those were the days before in-to-out! Consequently few players could get any draw on the ball, and mainly we just sliced our way around the course. Well, it took me a good twenty years to learn to correct that natural tendency in my own game, and then I had to learn to pass it on to my pupils. For make no mistake, everyone *has* to be taught; it does not come naturally. In some respects teaching golf is like fighting the Devil!

From the first time we see golf played to the first time we take a club in our hands, we have instinctively formed a false conception of the movement. We visualize the club head going up and over our shoulder and down onto the ball. You need only take any neophyte to see how he immediately takes the club up and down. His conviction that this is the correct movement is strengthened by the fact that he sees the ball soaring into the air and concludes that it must have been hit with an *upward* motion. So to make matters worse, he brings his hands into play also to assist the up-down-up movement—and is fully equipped for a career of scooping.

Now here are two devastatingly false impressions, and it is astonishing how long in many golfers' lives they remain. We must not try to lift either the club head or the ball, and we shall never be good golfers

The Feeling of In-to-Out

until we can feel that we pull the club head along as we swing, *along* not up and down.

Let us put this in another way. If I were to ask you to:
(1) Drive a wedge under a door
    and
(2) Drive a nail into the floor

—you would visualize two entirely different directions of hammer-head travel. Driving the wedge under the door is the direction we must feel at golf. The force must go along through the length of the wedge, along through the length of the ball.

With this in mind, it becomes clear that in swinging, the weight of the club head should be brought along from behind the ball, not from above it. This is what we call the wide swing, *wide* not high: a wide sweep that brings the club head in from behind the back of the ball.

Now another impression we get which impedes progress is that the club shaft goes up and above the right shoulder. In fact it does this not by arm or hand movement, but by the wrists being broken at the top of the swing. Consequently you must not try to get your club up by lifting it with your arms; you must feel at the top of the swing that your club and left arm are in a straight line and *are waist high*. Please ponder over this until you see its practical implications. You can try it out anywhere without a club and you will find that, if you are standing well up and your body is

On Learning Golf

braced and you have the straight-left-arm-waist-high feeling referred to above, you will *not be able* to hit in a downward direction, but you *will* be able to swing the club head along through the ball—with power from feet and legs.

Now unless you have corrected your natural misconceptions of the golf movement by experience, you will have another feeling at the top of the swing. You will feel that the best you can do from such a position will be to drag the ball along the ground a matter of fifty yards or so! And because you have this powerless feeling, you try to help the club head down with arms and hands—this is "hitting from the top," one of the cardinal sins of golf.

The reason why you have this feeling of insufficiency (until experience has corrected it) is that the wide sweeping swing which comes in from behind the ball and drags it forward gives you no sensation of speed, and speed you feel you must have! The secret of this lies in the fact that speed of swing and speed of club head are entirely different, and oddly enough it is the *slow* swing which, by enabling the wrists to open at the correct instant, gives you maximum club head speed where you want it—beyond the ball.

The difficulty of accepting this is that it is opposed to the natural instincts raised by our desire to hit a long way. We feel we want club head speed so we must swing fast, not realizing that the maximum speed can only come when the momentum of the club head is

OUT

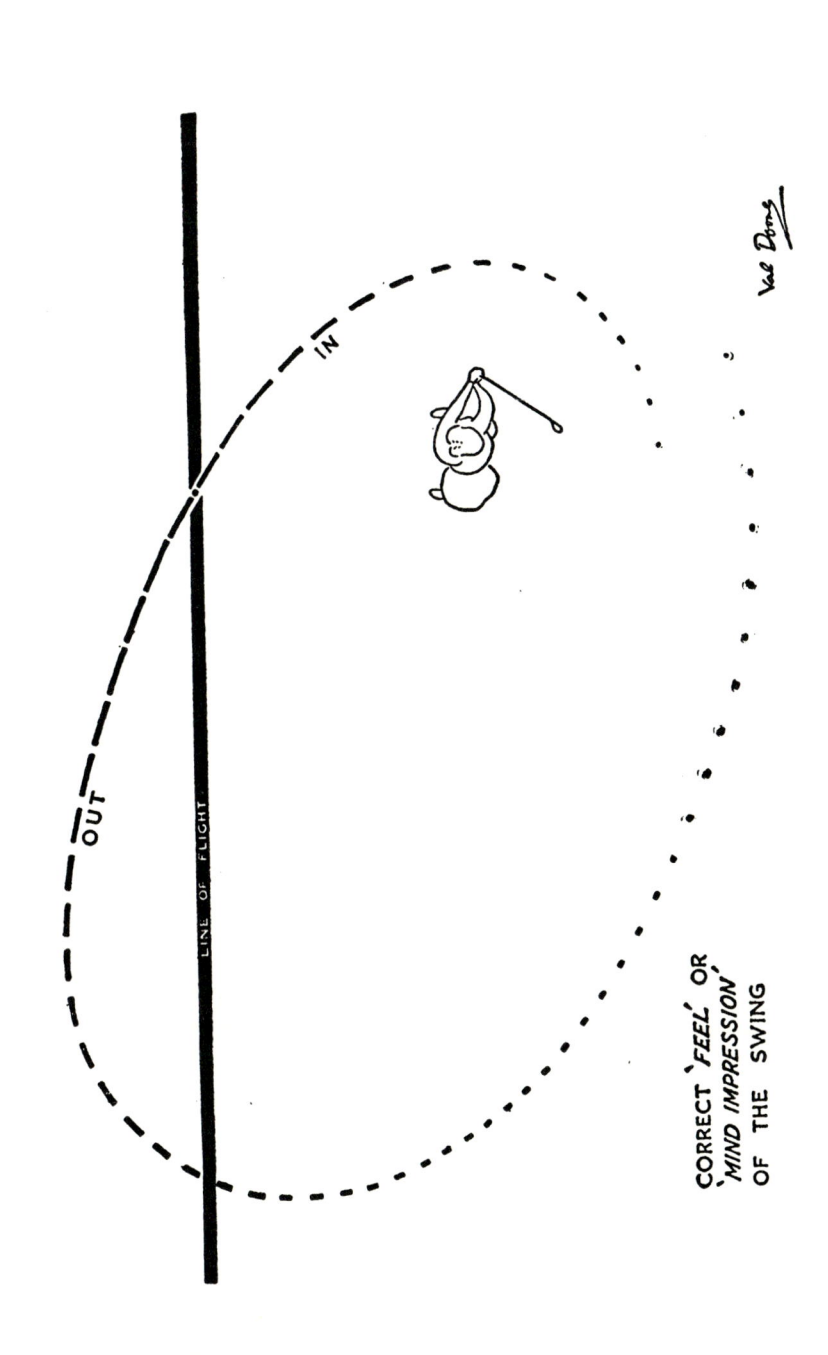

LINE OF FLIGHT

IN

CORRECT 'FEEL' OR
'MIND IMPRESSION'
OF THE SWING

Val Doms

On Learning Golf

free from our interference, when our opening wrists give it the speed and power of the *flail*. That is why I tell you that there is no such thing as a good natural golf swing. The natural swinger is the golf rabbit!

This sort of contradiction in the interests of efficiency is not exclusive to golf. Consider swimming. Doubtless the original "crawl" stroke was natural; its development is unnatural as anyone who watches it taught can see.

Please do not think that I have forgotten that the subject of the chapter is the in-to-out feeling. That feeling is a somewhat subtle one, and it can only be induced by getting certain details of the swing right. So I must dwell upon these details. The direction of swing was the first and now the source of power is the second.

I have told you not to use your arms to hit with, that in fact you should not play golf with your hands and arms at all but with your feet and legs. Now this is an exaggeration but one that is necessary to correct the natural tendency to use our hands and arms to the detriment of foot and leg work. The arms want to work and *will* work, so it is necessary to emphasize the importance of foot and leg action in order to get proper balance. Also it is true that movement *should start* in the feet and legs.

Of course the arms and hands play an essential part in transmitting this power to the ball. So, if we are told that we "are hitting with the right hand" and are ad-

The Feeling of In-to-Out

vised to correct this by holding less tightly with our right hand, we merely diminish our chance of hitting a long ball. The long ball feels to come out of the right hand, but the power that gives it comes from the feet, the legs, and the hips.

So it is obvious that the proper use of the legs and hips is essential if we are to pull the club head in correctly—at terrific speed into the back of the ball. Since action and reaction must be equal and opposite, we must pull *against* something, against some resistance. So at the top of the swing we must feel braced and very firmly set on the ground.

In a tug-of-war we can only use our weight and strength if we are well anchored. Also when we watch a boat race we are apt to think that it is the *arms* that are propelling the boat when actually it is the legs. But in both these cases the movement is simple, because force is applied directly along the line of flight. Much of the difficulty of golf arises because the source of power (our body) is *not* in the line of flight but is away to one side of it—so we have to produce our power and use our weight *by rotation*. We are a coiled spring, wound up by our rotation, and the heavier and more powerful the spring, the greater the force that will be implanted into the back of the ball when we "unwind" onto it. Also the greater the resistance that requires to be set up to give the spring secure anchorage. That is why it is that the farther you drive, the more important "brace" becomes.

On Learning Golf

Brace is important here for another reason also. You will remember that it is brace in general—and the several directions of brace in particular—that hold you in such a position and condition that you feel you are "inwards and behind the back of the ball." From this position, and swinging not up and down but around and along, you will find that the swing that feels to be taking the club head from in-to-out becomes not only possible but natural.

So you see that we have achieved this essential feel *not* by trying to force your club head in the direction you know you should feel it go, but by adapting a set and a conception of the correct direction of the golf movement that produces it as the natural, the almost inevitable result.

CHAPTER XIV

The Force-Center

I THINK that few experienced golfers will disagree with the dictum of that great teacher Ernest Jones that our strivings to attain a good swing will have been largely in vain unless at the end we have learned "to feel our club head."

Now this is a difficult thing to feel and an exceedingly difficult thing to teach a pupil to feel, though I have often succeeded in teaching it. The real difficulty is that you cannot teach it by teaching skill in the physical movements of the swing—yet this physical skill is a basic necessity before the feel can be induced. So we have to build up the good swing and then seek for "the feel of the club head" somewhere in its cycle.

We can pick this feel out most easily with the shorter clubs. Their heads are relatively heavy and the short shaft restricts the swing. It was with the No. 5 mashie that I personally first detected this feel. Incidentally, I should hate to tell you how long I had played golf before I did really feel that the club had a head to it! Very, very few of us feel the club head right from the time we walk up to address the ball until it fades away over our shoulder. In some great players this feel is so pronounced that you can actually see them seeking it

On Learning Golf

and using it. Walter Hagen approaching and on a tee was a lovely example of this and so today is Henry Cotton—no other modern player gives so strong an impression of club head feel as does Cotton in his drive. For though the feel is most easily detected in ourselves with the shorter clubs, its presence in others is most easily recognized in the full swing of the drive.

Now after years of study of this matter of club head feel, I came to a very curious conclusion about it, and it was this conclusion which enabled me to be quite exceptionally successful in imparting club head feel to my pupils. Here it is: we do not feel our club head with our hands; we feel it with our bodies.

What I mean is that, though the hands, being the "railhead" of our feel, do of course play an important part, yet the feel does not stay in them—the hands (and arms of course, though less consciously) *transmit this feel to the body* to the central organization of our golf mechanism. And arising from this the most common mistake we make in trying to feel the club head is to look for the feeling of it in our hands instead of at the center.

This matter of feel at the center is so important that I have coined a name for its seat, for where it is felt. I call it the "force-center." I cannot give you an exact anatomical definition of where the force-center *is*, because its position varies with different shots. As the shot (and the swing) become *longer*, so the force-center rises; as they become shorter, the position of

134

The Force-Center

the force-center drops. Yet there is always the feeling that we swing from a center, wherever that center may be. And where it is, there also must be the feel of the club head.

Having reached this conclusion as to the location of club head feel, it was easy to see why this is the most difficult of golfing feels to develop and the easiest to lose touch with. Between the club head and the force-center there are a number of connections in the swing (such as the wrists and the shoulders), and should any of these connections be broken, should our swing become disjointed, then the feeling of the club head cannot be transmitted back to the force-center.

This breakup of the swing most usually occurs towards the top of the swing, where we can lose connection by breaking the left arm at the elbow or by opening the hands—two very simple and common mechanical faults. When I began to realize the relationship between a connected swing and club head feel I found a curious thing, that my driving swing was cut down automatically to three-quarters. Incidentally an excellent illustration of the importance of a *right conception*!

The more you study it, the more you will see that the modern three-quarters swing is simply a *connected* swing and that the three-quarters is the limit of the swing because it is the limit to which most of us can go without breaking the connections. When first I came to this conclusion, I went to as many Championships as I

135

On Learning Golf

could and watched the boys and tried to pick out those who followed my idea of swinging from a connected center and those who did not. One thing that I noticed at once was that the connected swingers—so-called controlled swingers—were always firmer and slower, the quicker swingers were less controlled and their swings were more liable to come unstuck. Also I noticed that as a general rule the controlled swingers did not hold their wrists down as they addressed the ball; they held them *up* in a line with the arm and club shaft.

Now that was an interesting point, and when I tried it out, I found that it had an important bearing on the whole matter. This position of the wrists gives us at once the feeling of the *club head* being *down*. Please note this is a *club head* feeling. This particular feeling, club head *down* at the address, has always been recognized as part of the correct golf feel. Our forefathers told us to keep our wrists down as we addressed the ball through a misapprehension of it; they felt *down* when they hit a good shot and thought it was their wrists that were down, whereas it was really the *club head*.

Because of that initial misconception, they had to make corrections and compensations on the way up and on the way down, but we can now eliminate these and make the swing more simple. The fewer unnecessary movements you make in a swing the better. A simple swing always has been and always will be desir-

The Force-Center

able; so I aim at eliminating every unnecessary movement—and I can assure you I got rid of a big one when I concluded that the wrists should not be held down, yet the club head should feel down. Try to get this nuance, it is important.

If you try and compare these two feelings with a club, you will find you can push the club head down on the turf *with the sole flat* but not when the toe is cocked up in the air. This sole flat and down is the right feel. You see, golf force is centrifugal so the arms *must* be at full stretch when we come into the region of the ball, and we can only get this full stretch down at the foot of the swing if we feel *down* right through the swing.

I remember telling this to a pupil of mine, a good pupil in the sense that he was a good analyst, and he looked at me in astonishment. "Do you mean that I have to feel *down* when I am at the top of my swing?" he asked. "You do," I replied. He said nothing at the time, but one day later he said to me suddenly, "I can feel that down feeling when I am up now and by George! I like it! It keeps me beautifully down to the bottom of the ball automatically." The *automatically* was what I liked.

"But," you may say, "as I address the ball with my club head on the ground behind it, I must naturally feel down." Not necessarily. Feeling down is connected with the correct brace of the body. You will never feel down if you slouch over the ball; the feel-

On Learning Golf

ing comes by opposing the club head by bracing the body. You must push down *against* something, and the down feeling is the feeling that you are braced upward against the club head as it is down behind the ball.

The first thing I do with a new pupil is to kneel on the ground and hold his club head and ask him to pull against it. I ask him to hold his position and then relax my pressure, and he at once feels what it is to feel pushing down. This is the feeling he must get as he comes into contact with the ball—which is why I repeat and keep on repeating, "Full stretch, full stretch all the time!" Even as you go through the ball you must feel down; "down while through the ball" is an exquisite golf feel.

So much for one end of the feel! What about the other end, the force-center? This is obviously a difficult feel to fix, and the best way I have found is by making the pupil stand in the imaginary barrel described in the chapter on the "Swing." You will remember that swinging in this barrel gives him the feeling of keeping his hips up; at the same time he must now *stretch down* (even when his hands are up chest high). Because the body is braced, there will no longer be any tendency for the knees to sag in towards one another; they will roll round at a constant height as he pivots and this is a very essential feel in the back swing.

Now we are building up so that you will shortly be able to feel your force-center, but first another word

The Force-Center

or two about the hips. The feel of holding them up that you get through the barrel image is a good one. So is the sort of hip brace you can get by pulling your hips in as you walk. I often tell pupils to do this. You get the feeling of holding your hips firmly together and that they no longer sag or dip first to the right and then to the left.

The good swing is based on a pivot with the minimum of to-and-fro movement. Both hips and shoulders are held up and braced, and they move in the same circular path—except that the turn of the body slightly inclines the shoulders as they go round. Now if you stand before an imaginary ball, holding an imaginary club, with your arms stretched down but held lightly (with little tension, I mean) as if you were ready to play a shot, and then turn first right and then left, rather briskly and getting the movement from the knees, calves, and feet, you will begin to feel the pull on your arms from the force-center. *The power is largely produced by the feet and legs, but it is the force-center (somewhere in the pit of the back) which collects it and is responsible for its transfer to the arms and then out to the club head.*

Now take a mashie and do very short swings to and fro with it. Soon you will begin to detect the *center* which you will feel controls both the setting up of power and the guiding of the club. Do not break the wrists or lift the club head during this experiment. The hands do nothing but keep the club straight out in

139

On Learning Golf

front of you; let the arms feel supple and yet pushed down as the club head is down, while all the time you are moving to and fro from the legs. You begin to feel connected right through, from legs to center and from center to club head. Though you make this experiment first with a mashie (that being an easy club to feel), the full drive is simply a big edition of the same movement and must be just as connected.

What I think you will find different in this braced pivot movement as compared with an uncontrolled swing is this: as your hips turn without sag, you will feel you are getting more power and getting it in a different way. You develop rotary power, largely from the legs. This is what I want you to feel, because, when you feel it, you may know that you have got your nether regions well fixed in space.

Now we have to find a similar fixing for the shoulders, to control their position and direction of movement. How should they be held at the address and what is their movement? You have to incline them forward slightly as you address the ball, but see that it is *only* slightly, only as little as your build makes necessary. And keep them both up; especially keep the left shoulder up as you go back and the right shoulder up as you come through.

Just as the barrel has made your hips turn horizontally, with no sway, so should your shoulders feel that they turn horizontally. You can if you wish imagine a hoop from the barrel holding them in place. They

The Force-Center

will swing freely in this without touching it, but in a slightly inclined plane because of the forward bend of the body. But my own method of fixing the shoulders is different. It is to feel that there is a direct connection between the left heel and the right shoulder, a diagonal tie that keeps them connected and at an unvarying distance one from the other, as we go up, as we come down, and as we follow through.

This is a difficult connection to describe, but once you have grasped its full meaning you will realize its value. As we lift our left heel—going back—we will (if the tie is properly realized) feel our right shoulder move back in response. The shoulder and heel keep their distance, never getting closer or farther away; so when the left heel comes *down,* we will feel the right shoulder moving forward in a straight line against the ball—neither dipping under it nor rising over it. This is right.

The right shoulder should never feel to *dip under the ball,* though it should be felt to go down to it. As we can see when we look at the "flickers," it is true that the right shoulder *is* lower than the left as we strike the ball, but so it is at the address—and there must be no more feel of it being lower at the moment of impact than there is at the address.

In fact the feel of the shoulder movement in a correctly braced swing is that the shoulders move round *parallel to the ground.*

Now when you have got this diagonal tie working

On Learning Golf

and can give a peep at it and at your hip brace at the same time, you will feel properly compact and *centered* as you swing. And it is only when you feel yourself to be centered that you can hope to feel the club head as you should.

For, please remember that all this discussion of brace and connections is relative to the feel of the club head. As I told you, you can only get this feel reliably at your force-center, and unless you build up a force-center by brace and connections, you will not feel it properly at all. For in the uncontrolled *natural* swing there is no force-center; that primarily is what is the matter with such a swing: too many separate forces are working independently in it.

So I have told you how to build up a force-center, and that when you have built it up, you should be able to feel the club head in it. You will be able to do this only if there is no break in the connections between the club head and the force-center, but one of these connections—the arms—is the most liable to disconnection of any in the whole swing.

At first glance this would seem easy enough to control, because the arms should work in exact relation to the shoulders and chest. The thorax and biceps should become one in movement. But things do not work out this way, because we do inherently—and in spite of ourselves—consider golf as being played with the arms. So we *use* our arms, ever so little it may be but enough

The Force-Center

to make us disconnected. Now this is a fine and most delicate point in which lies most of the difference between a good, a very good, and a superlative golfer. It is by the management of the arms that championships are won and lost.

For it is no use to have built up perfect connections to bring co-ordination to the whole body throughout the whole swing if we then *break* the connection at a vital point by allowing our arms to work independently of our chest and shoulders. They must be not independent but reactive. The body in the swing must be a unity.

Now at first we are likely to find ourselves contradicting this idea of unity at some point or other, because we will probably have one or two points of *feel* that do not seem to fit into the scheme. But give your muscles a little experience of the new movements required of them and they will soon settle down. Then you will go on from day to day, testing new feels—rejecting some but *accepting* those which fit into your swing. So you will become more and more clear about the feeling of a good swing.

I must remind you again, because it is fundamental to this book, that *learning by a sense of feel* is something quite different to learning by the intellect. Intellectual memory may be of use in learning golf but it is never paramount. What is paramount is what I have called muscular memory, a memory for the right *feel-*

On Learning Golf

ing of a movement which enables the muscles to repeat that movement time after time, without directions from brain or will.

What I have been trying to do in this book, and I can assure you it is no easy task, is to put on paper a method whereby you can pull the ends of your swing together and get it all properly connected. But when you have done this, it is up to you to make yourself so familiar with the feel of your controlled swing that you can produce it automatically, practically by reflex action, whenever you like.

But I warn you again that a single break in the connections will render the success of a shot a matter of chance, whereas you want it to be a matter of certainty. You know the type of player who has to depend upon his lucky day—disconnected! He *can* produce a good swing or he would never have a lucky day; he cannot produce it regularly because he loses connection somewhere. And the chances are that he loses it by *using his arms*. And *why* does he start using his arms? Ninety-nine times out of a hundred because he tries too hard to hit the ball!

Yes, it is usually Golf Bogey No. 1 which induces us to use our arms. That overwhelmingly common-sense impulse to *hit* the ball where we want it to go. And how can we hit *but* with our arms? So, all our carefully-contrived controls go overboard, and we take vicious scoops and lashes at the ball.

What a pity! *What* a pity! For if we had inhibited

The Force-Center

our desire to hit the ball and concentrated upon producing a perfect swing—power from the pivot, shoulder controlled by heel movement, arms acting reactively to the shoulders, wrists free for the flail—we would have sent it twice as far and straighter. And we should have felt the club head in our power center and have known that we had the secret of successful golf.

CHAPTER XV

Interlude for Instruction

o

MONOLOGUE

"OH, good morning, Mr. Boomer.—You *are* Mr. Boomer, aren't you? . . . I'm Mrs. de Vere de Vere; you know, Mrs. Pro Quid Quo sent me along to you, to get my swing fixed up. . . . Nothing much, but of course you know I'm an old golfer; so I'd better tell you all about my case. Possibly you have met my husband somewhere . . . he has played golf all his life more or less . . . plays very well too; no *style*, you know, but hits a very long ball and plays his irons to perfection . . . and his putting, my dear fellow, you should *see* his putting; it's marvellous. You see, he was taught by that St. Andrews Pro . . . famous chap. . . ."

"Kirkcaldy?" I suggested.

"Yes, that's the fellow. People say he is funny. I can't see it. . . . I did have one lesson from him, but I didn't get his humor at all. . . . *Gruff*, I thought he was; good with the men, no doubt, but *not* with ladies. . . . We *do* like a little finesse, you know . . . still he did say I had a style like Vardon's—or was it a grip? . . . and he said something about a greyhound, too. I put that down to my being fond of coursing, but of course he may have meant it as a compliment to my figure

Monologue

... they *do* like to pay you a compliment every now and then just to encourage you."

"Oh!" was all I had time to ejaculate.

"Oh yes. . . . Now it appears that I have a very special swing; so naturally I don't want you to alter it . . . of course, I never could pivot or keep the left arm straight or any of that elementary stuff you tell beginners . . . but they tell me—at least, Lord Brownseed told me . . . you know, that plus three gentleman who nearly beat Jobby Bones once in the championship . . . well, he told me I had a most perfect and delicate grip . . . 'something worth contemplating' was his phrase . . . he sings you know . . . between you and me, I think he is a bit poetical. . . . Well, as I was going to say . . ."

She paused for an instant as she caught sight of the caddy, who was having a snooze out in the rough; then she was off again—

"Well . . . as I was saying, I've hardly played at all since I played at North Berwick last year . . . no, not last year, two summers ago. I had a few tips there from old Ned Redwood . . . you know him; at least he knows you, and thinks a lot of you too . . . he said he wouldn't mind handing me over to you. He beat you once, didn't he? . . . he tells the story very well; we had it for dinner one evening, stroke by stroke, and it lasted five courses! But I remember that the family didn't seem over-interested, as if they had heard it before . . . maybe they had; Ned is getting on, and

On Learning Golf

one is apt to repeat oneself . . . as that rude comedian Bobbie said about sardines. Personally I don't like them, sardines I mean, . . . but as a matter of fact he is quite right about them. . . . Oh yes, I was coming to this. I developed a simply *terrific* slice . . . you wouldn't believe! Now let me get it right. I know how particular you silly Pros are about details. . . . Yes, it was at Gullane on No. 1 course—or was it No. 2? . . . numbers are so confusing and there are so many courses there, you know, I get quite lost. . . . Anyway I remember the *day* because I had a caddy, *such* a cute little chap . . . and quick—he had a sort of second sight, and more than once he was half-way down the street after my ball before I had hit it . . . and every time he retrieved it before it got as far as Wack Jite's shop. That's the best of always having the same caddy . . . they get to know your style and it saves you money, in Scotland, anyway."

"But . . ." I tried to edge in.

"Oh yes, of course, my slice! . . . Well, someone gave me a very simple bit of advice—was it Ned or was it Tyril Solley? . . . you would know because you know their styles. Anyway, they said, "turn your left hand a little more over the back of the shaft and bring your left foot back a little"—whoever it was who told me, and I still think it was Ned. Hey presto! I not only cured my slice but pulled my ball slap into the rough on the left. . . . I must admit that the rough on the left is no better than the rough on the right, but

Monologue

the moral effect was astounding. . . . Do you know, we actually won 5 and 4 that day, which only shows how simple it is when one knows."

"Knows what?" I queried, mesmerized.

"That's just it," she continued. "It's so difficult to meet simple people. Do you know what one fellow told me? . . . you don't mind, do you, but he was a Pro . . . but there, I always say that all Pros are not alike; some are better brought up than others . . . present company excepted, of course! But the Hon. Billy Bunk told me such a good story which he read in Simpson's book about the Pro who taught Balfour—the Premier, you know . . . fine man, Balfour; *he* wouldn't have let things get so complicated, my husband says. . . . Oh, where was I?"

"The Pro," I suggested.

"Oh yes, the story Billy told, only it was really Simpson's story, of course, was that one of them said . . . I forget if it was the Pro or Balfour . . . that, 'the ground on which golf is played is called links. Links are too broken for cultivation; but sheep, rabbits, geese, and professionals pick up a precarious livelihood on them' . . . you don't mind, do you . . . it's so *true*."

"Especially about the geese," I said.

"Well, now, where was I? Oh, the fellow who told me, told me not to open the face of the club as I took it back, and yet, do you know, my husband says that the first thing Vardon told him was to open the face of the club as he went back . . . it just shows, doesn't it?

On Learning Golf

. . . then poor old Ned asked Totton why he opened the face of his club on the way back and Totton told him not to ask silly questions . . . devastating wasn't it?—or so my hubby says."

"Who really taught you, Madam?" I got in.

"Oh, how *silly* of me. . . . I quite forgot you would want to know that. . . . You know, last summer, I think it was, we went to Gleneagles for the week, and on the way back we stayed a day or two in London and had a lovely week-end out at Sir Bunsen Burner's place—some Park—Lent Park, is it?—such lovely daffodils—only they were over then, of course . . . and there is a dinky little course there . . . you must know it."

"Yes, I do."

"They have a special Burgundy there . . . my goodness, but there's a fine drink—not good for the tip of your nose, of course . . . but what's powder for anyway? Yet, would you believe it?—there was a woman in the party who said she made *her* Burgundy by tipping a glass of port into a carafe of *vin rouge ordinaire*. . . . As a matter of fact I tried it myself later on some not important guests, and it came off . . . anyway, it went down!"

"So when you were at Lent Park, I suppose you had a lesson from Skeet?"

"Oh no . . . we had no time . . . only a few hours . . . so I had my lesson at a school, in London . . . Park Street, was it? . . . anyway, the Pro there is a

Monologue

very definite kind of chap . . . 'straight arm' and all that elementary stuff. I really didn't take to him . . . he was so cocksure of himself, which is silly when you only know 'beginners' style,' isn't it? . . . Anyway I only had one lesson because he nearly pulled my arm out of its socket. Do you know, it made me so stiff all down the left side that I had to walk out of the bloody place sideways."

"Oh," I gurgled, pushing a fit back into my throat.

"What's that funny noise?" she inquired. "Sounds like a squirrel. . . . Do you have squirrels here? . . . you have such *lovely* trees. Are they natural? . . ."

"No," I said, "it wasn't a squirrel. It was probably the caddy having a day-dream."

"How silly of me! I forgot the caddy. Oh yes, now I remember what I came for. Someone told me you have a wonderful theory . . . just the thing for me, they assured me."

"Who told you that?" I asked suspiciously.

"Well, it's difficult to say. . . . You see, we had you at a knitting-bee . . . an all-hen show, of course. If you had heard all they said about you, you would have blushed . . . *do* you blush? Anyway, one woman told us you put a hundred yards on her drive, and another that you got her handicap down 15 strokes in as many days . . . one stout old dowager declared you had made her pitch better with her eyes shut than she did with them open . . . and there was that American woman—dames they call them, don't they?—she was

On Learning Golf

upset with you because you taught her how to play stymies, and then the Ambassador told her they didn't play stymies any more in the States . . . yet you know she had roped in three perfectly good husbands in her time . . . and *none* of them paupers! Strange, isn't it?"

"No," I said just to see what would happen.

"What do you mean. . . . 'No'!" she said, with such alacrity that I took it back.

"Sorry—I should have said, 'Yes.' But what about your swing, Madam?—Time is getting on."

"Oh yes—we really must. You see, I can't hit a ball. Put me down a peg, will you, and I will take a few swings."

She took a few swings—or, more precisely, swipes. They told me all I needed to know.

"Madam," I said, "who am I to meddle with such a swing? . . . As your friend said, it's something to contemplate. . . . Only don't say Percy Boomer told you so, please . . . my regular pupils might become jealous. But there *is* one thing I would like to ask you before I go on to my next pupil, and it might help you if you could answer."

"Well, what is it?"

"When Ned told you to turn your left hand more over the back of the shaft and to draw your left foot back a bit, you say it worked at first. Now are you sure, *quite* sure, that he did not say *right* foot?"

She paused, she gaped, she gasped.

Monologue

"Why how *stupid* of me! . . . of course it was my right foot. . . . What a *lucky* thing you thought of asking me such a stupid question. You don't mind, do you, but of course it *was* stupid. Of course it was my right foot, as I said . . ."

NEARING THE FINISH

POINTS OF STUDY

The impression here is of the arms stretching upwards . . . but the essential *feel* of the *arms stretching down through the ball* is retained.

The hips have turned almost horizontally. They are braced together, the left hip has not been thrown out.

The weight of the body has not been completely transferred to the left foot, the left leg is slanting slightly back, and in consequence weight is still being taken by the big toe of the right foot.

The right leg and hip are twisted inwards: hence the fine vertical balance of the whole movement.

The hands are almost closed, as they were at the address (very important). The wrists are close together.

The shoulders are almost horizontal.

NEARING THE FINISH

AUBREY

CHAPTER XVI

Rhythm

IT took me a long time to make up my mind to write this chapter, and now as I sit down to begin it I am appalled by the huge gaps in my train of thought. In fact I would like another twenty years or so to think it over in, before writing about it at all.

But that will not do, because it is no use trying to write an intelligent book on golf and leaving rhythm out, for rhythm is the very soul of golf. So I must do the best I can, and in this chapter I will endeavor to tell you what I have discovered to date about rhythm in relation to golf. And that is not going to be easy with such an abstract and subtle subject, so I ask your indulgence.

Rhythm we know in ordinary circumstances as *flowing motion,* and in golf this resolves itself into *timed movements.* Let us start with an exceedingly practical example of what this means. The most accepted theory is that as the club head approaches the ball your wrists will flick or become taut. When? you ask. That has really never been defined, and the best definition I know of it is, "co-ordination of mind and muscle which enables the player to do exactly the right thing at the proper moment" . . . so you must find your own rhythm.

On Learning Golf

So we can start from the familiar word "timing," which is an advantage. But though every golfer knows the word, fewer appreciate the significance of the sense which it represents. Because until timing does become a *sense* with us, a sense of something *rhythmic*, our attempts at co-relating movements can only be on a very crude mechanical basis. It is stretching the phrase to talk of the "rhythm" by which a self-change gear box shifts gears, but a soaring seagull is charged with rhythm at its highest. The trouble with golf is that we are gear boxes trying to become seagulls. We have to develop rhythm on a mechanical base.

We want rhythm, flowing movement, in our swing. But as we have already discovered we have to dissect our swing before we can play it—just as a musician has to dissect a composition before he can even play the notes. And please note that he may learn to play the notes and *nothing more;* that is he may never get as far as the rhythm and tone in which all the delicate beauty and meaning of music are hidden. So also with our swings: we may have memorized the mechanics faultlessly and be able to perform them time after time, but, unless they can be blended by rhythm into a perfectly timed flowing whole, it will be a poor sort of soulless mechanical golf which we play. For, to repeat, *rhythm is the soul of golf.*

When we watch a really good golfer, we are impressed, of course, by the beauty of his swing, but perhaps even more by the sensation of *prolonged effortless*

Rhythm

flight which his shots produce on us. They seem unaffected by the force of gravity, whereas our own poor efforts make for the earth at the earliest possible moment, which—as one of my pupils brightly suggested—may be why bad golfers are dubbed rabbits!

The good golfer can make the ball do two things which the bad or merely indifferent golfer cannot make it do.

(1) The good golfer can make the ball remain in the air a long time in the drive, or run a long way in the putt.

(2) The good golfer can make the ball fly, or run, dead straight.

Now these two attributes of a good shot are due to a profound knowledge of the golf mechanics *plus* good timing. Since I have been at Sunningdale I have played often with a delightful old Blackheath golfer, Mr. A.T. Turquand Young—father of the great English Rugby forward. Though he is nearer eighty than seventy he is sweeping the ball off the tee perfectly, and, in addition to being academically faultless, his tee shots are almost as long as my own. His swing is an object lesson in effortless rhythm.

So one day I asked him to be so kind as to jot down how he came to swing so slowly and smoothly, how he came to get so far with so little effort. And did he play directly with his hands and arms? He gave me the following with permission to include it in this book.

"At the age of sixteen I found out in two things that

On Learning Golf

'slow movement' beat 'force' every time. One was in throwing the hammer, the other was in throwing a cricket ball. As a result of this experience, I began to play golf with as slow a swing as possible, getting the power from below the waist with the result that without any effort I became a *very* long driver even in the gutty period.

"After a lapse of some years owing to illness I came back to the game just as good as when I left off, after an hour or so swinging with my clubs. The slow swing looks lazy, but the power is there and it certainly does *not* come from the arms and hands. Providing your back swing goes up all in one piece and your timing is correct, one can send the ball a very long way without effort. Of that there is no mistake, I know it from experience."

There you have it! Mr. Turquand Young found that "slow movement beat force every time." What a find—and what a grand age to make it at, sixteen!

Now as that story suggests, perfect mechanics alone are not sufficient in golf. Let us try and examine the effect of accurate *timing* and see *why* it makes such a difference—the difference which we can all recognize between the *almost* perfectly timed shot and the *perfectly* timed one.

It hinges upon the fact that golf is a *dead ball* game. We have to set the ball in motion from a state of rest and this largely accounts for the extraordinary complexity and subtlety of the game. Good shots are easier

Rhythm

to play in live ball games than they are in golf because the velocity at which the ball comes to us sets up a *rebound*, which together with the speed of the head of the implement we wield increases the speed of our return blow. The relationship of ball velocity, club velocity, and *rebound* are simplified.

Now we can trace the two elements of rebound and club head speed in the drive, the longest of golf shots. But now because the ball is "dead" their relationship is no longer simple. It is necessary to get the correct *proportion* of each of these elements into the stroke or the resultant shot will not be perfect. A slight overemphasis on either one or other of them completely changes the flight of the shot and such slight overemphasis in either direction is not a matter of golf mechanics but is due to a delicate inflection of *timing*.

Let us see how this arises. It is generally assumed that the faster we swing the club head through the ball, the longer the ball will be. This is true if, but *only* if, the maximum club head speed is attained just *after* we come into contact with the ball. Hence the fact that we often get exceptionally long shots when we are trying to hit easy ones. With the slower swing, the club head has still been *accelerating* when it made contact with the ball and so has been able to "stay longer with the ball" *and so make use of the rebound.*

We have timed a shot well only when we feel we have remained a long time in contact with the ball, "gathering it up and slinging it off the face of the club

On Learning Golf

head" as I have called it. If we are to do this, the club head must have sufficient power to take up the shock of impact *and still keep accelerating.* If at the moment of impact we stop the forward pull of the left side (which is what we will do if we aim at the ball), this power is not available and the club head cannot, as it should, continue accelerating in contact with the ball until the ball rebounds from it.

We have timed a shot well only when we feel we have remained a long time in contact with the ball. If we stop the forward pull of the left side at the moment of impact with the ball, we do not set up the resistance necessary to take up the shock of impact and *at the same time* to keep the club head accelerating until the ball rebounds from it. In fact if we let up on the forward pull when we strike the ball, we "stop the club head at the ball," an absolutely cardinal fault in swinging. That is why I always tell my pupils (and repeat it time after time in this book) *never try to hit the ball;* cultivate a sweep through the ball, and let the ball be nothing more than an incident in the swing.

Until you have built up your correct psychophysical reflexes to control Golf Bogey No. 1 you will have to use your will power not to try to hit the ball. Your club head has to sweep down and through, gathering speed progressively. But the climax of this acceleration, as I tell you, must be *not* at the ball but away past it. If we make the ball our center of attraction, our acceleration will culminate at that point, and since our

Rhythm

effort will be exhausted, we shall not be able to "stay with the ball."

Now I have found that people who feel like this do so because they *overswing*. Overswinging is the natural result of trying to hit the ball; the three-quarter swing is the natural result of trying to sweep through and past the ball. The three-quarter swing puts the natural climax of acceleration of the club head where it should be, about a yard past the ball, but if you go *back* too far, you will not be able to maintain acceleration to this point.

From which arises a curious and valuable illustration of teaching methods. As you know, I do not like simply to say to a pupil, "You came down outside," or "You are overswinging." These faults are mainly not mechanical at all; they arise from a *false conception*, and if I correct the false conception, the fault cures itself. In this case I found that the people who were overswinging were doing so because they were concentrating on the ball. When I had explained that the climax of acceleration must be a yard or so past the ball, their back swings began to shorten automatically —because they felt the need for a reserve of effort to enable them to go on past the ball.

In short the good golfer *measures the length of his back swing by the feel of his follow through.* He is not consciously aware how far back he goes but he *is* aware of the acceleration climax point away past the ball. This point *and not the ball* is the true center of the

On Learning Golf

swing, and obviously the farther *past* the ball it is placed, the shorter must the back swing be.

In passing, I may point out that the conception of the center of the swing being away past the ball explains the meaning of the instruction to "hit your mashie shots on the down swing." If you *try* to do that, you will land into trouble. When using your mashie, you simply put the ball nearer your right foot (because of the shorter club) and *again swing through the ball*, thus taking it on the down swing.

Timing, then, is: (1) The gathering up of speed through the ball from correct mechanical movement, and (2) a correct conception of the location of the swing center. These two can only be blended into a whole which can be faithfully repeated time after time by our sense of rhythm.

If, as we stand on the tee, I tell you to hum over the first two bars of the *Blue Danube* and then the first two bars of the *Sailor's Hornpipe,* you will get the sense of two quite different rhythms. You will not find it difficult to recognize which is the rhythm of the slow, flowing swing—which it is that Mme Lacoste used when each spring we went out together to play a few shots to tune her swing up. She it was who told me that if she found herself swinging too quickly, this rhythm would put her right again immediately. Incidentally until your own rhythm is well established, it is liable to be affected by that of those you play with. One of the reasons why Mme Lacoste

Rhythm

finds a few holes with me a good tuning-up process is that my own swinging rhythm is very similar to her own.

Now we must go into the question of contact with the club through the hands. I know that this is a chapter on rhythm not on grip, but ninety-nine times out of a hundred when we break up the rhythm of a swing we do it *by using our hands wrongly*.

My own grip is a variation of Vardon's, with only two knuckles of the left hand showing and three of the right hand. My left hand is not turned over the shaft and the right is very much on top. As my wrists are fully up as I address the ball, I feel as if I am pointing a revolver down at it and *my trigger finger is waiting for the trigger pull*. Obviously if you use a different grip, you will experience a somewhat different *feel*. Personally I find that the trigger finger of my right hand plays a great part in my rhythm. The right-hand power, which we feel (mainly in the trigger finger) as we come into contact with the ball, must be induced by resistance set up in the body, *not* by forward force set up by the right hand. For though the *feel* of golf may be largely right-handed, the power of golf is centrifugal.

Next, we will never get effective rhythm into our swings unless we have a proper conception of that word "wait" or, as I have told you I now prefer, "delay."

I have told you that I dislike "wait" because it seems

On Learning Golf

to imply stopping, and stopping breaks up the flow or rhythm of the swing. I used to wonder *what* I was to wait for and when and how it would catch me up. The club head perhaps? But what would it catch up?—the body? If so, if we stop the body at the ball and allow the hands to catch up, we make a direct hit at the ball which we know to be wrong.

So I analyzed it out to this conclusion: We begin the up swing all in a piece and naturally our leg and foot and hip movements are completed long before our wrists are fully broken back at the top, long before the club head begins its return journey. Since we must keep our feet, legs, and hips moving smoothly, they get far ahead of the club head. We actually *encourage* this gap by not clinging tight onto the club with our hands, but leaving our wrists flexible. What we are waiting for is the *return power,* the forward pull of the body that pulls the right hand and throws the club shaft back onto the trigger finger.

We must *not* intentionally pull with the right hand, we must wait for the body to pull it. We take up the feel of this pull mainly with our trigger finger; in a strong player the resistance may be so terrific as to burst the finger open.

So we delay while all the time we are going forward. We are *waiting in movement.*

You will now see why I explained my grip to you in some detail. But the regulated succession of movements is the same in every good swing, the point of

Rhythm

contact (in my case the trigger finger) being the varying factor. The detail of the grip is important only in that it must have a point of contact and resistance. This can be and often is in the left hand, but I personally much prefer my own grip which I have developed out of vast experience from the so-called Vardon grip. Perhaps I should add that although I have what might be termed a family affection for this grip—for was not the genial Harry a pupil of my father?—the reason why I adopted it is simply that it is the best suited to giving you the sense of connection between *power* and *feel*.

You will realize that in developing my ideas on rhythm in golf I have come up against many interesting points which are not immediately obvious. I remember telling a pupil of mine the *Blue Danube* story. "Oh," she said, "do you really believe the ear has an influence upon golf rhythm?" Well did I? I suppose I did, as I told the story in all sincerity, but I had not thought the point out. The actual sound of a "swishing" swing cutting the daisies is different and suggests a different rhythm from the "sweeping" sound of a good shot.

The swishing sensation of the daisy cutter is too directly a simple one-two sensation; the sensation of the sweeping shot includes *drag* (from the "wait" or "delay"). When the Americans say they put draw on the ball (in English, impart a slight *pull*) they swing the ball slightly from right to left at the end of its flight. That is the result of the feeling that we are

On Learning Golf

drawing the ball in. This is the basis of the in-to-out theory; we feel that, as we come in behind the ball, the club head goes *out* with a corresponding reaction by the ball in flight.

As I have suggested, I do not think either "pull" or "draw" suggests the right sensation. *Drag* suggests it much more nearly. A horse *pulls* a cart, a car *draws* a trailer (directly linked in each case) but we *drag* a fishing net, or a kite. In short, if we want to draw the ball, we must *drag* the club head. We drag the club head *in order to* draw the ball.

But you may say, "What has drag to do with rhythm?" It has all to do with it, with our feeling of flowing continuous movement.

Golf rhythm is a delayed dragging feel of the club head, developed from the power of the legs, kept under control by the braced turning of the hips, and finally loosened into a free, untrammeled movement of the arms outward and around the left side.

If to this we add a sense of balance, a sense of unhurried calm, a feeling that there is lots of time to feel each movement blending into the others, we shall begin to feel the true golf rhythm. We must swing slowly yet determinedly. When children are lost in the dark, they hurry; when *we* are lost in our swing, *we* hurry! This rhythmic swing seems slow, seems to take a long time to develop. We must cultivate this feeling and see slowly and feel slow. We lose rhythm as soon as we hurry, and we hurry as soon as we are afraid.

Rhythm

The fear complex beats every golfer at some time of his playing career. Don't mind admitting it; you will be in gallant company—the late Lord Beatty told me at St. Cloud in 1920 that every man is a coward when he steps onto a golf course!

THE GOLF SWING IN EMBRYO

POINTS TO STUDY

For *all* golfers the most important picture in the book to study.

Above the line all movement is passive, below the line it is active.

Leg muscles have been used to push out the left knee and to pull back the right knee. No other muscle in the whole body has been used *actively*.

Relative to the club, the hips, shoulders, arms, and hands are in exactly the same position as at the address.

Conversely, to bring everything back to the position of the address, all that needs to be done is to straighten the left leg and slightly to bend the right one.

The reason for keeping the wrists *up* at the address is now obvious. Had they been broken (held *down*) at the address they would be cocked up as the club was carried back.

THE GOLF SWING IN EMBRYO

PERCY

CHAPTER XVII

Interlude for Instruction

AS A DANCER SEES IT

I NEVER consider I have succeeded with a pupil unless the pupil adds something to my own knowledge. A pupil who teaches me nothing has no originality, since what I am trying to impart is *sensation* and surely no two people should *feel* with exact similarity. So I encourage my pupils to talk and give their impressions of things, particularly of *feels*, and my experience is that if these impressions are banal neither the pupil nor I will learn anything! On the other hand, a pupil may come along with some quite absurd or fantastic conception of what I have tried to explain—and then I know there is fertility and that it is up to me to get a crop of ideas out of it.

So I felt I had a chance to do some good work when one day a well-known dance instructress came to me to be re-taught. Here was someone who, in addition to being intelligent, had spent her life in attaining reflex movements in their highest and most beautiful form and in learning to impart such movements to others.

Not that it does to be too optimistic in these matters. I had taught dancers before and one of the greatest of these had evolved the most completely unbalanced swing you ever set eyes on. Also I had given golf les-

On Learning Golf

sons to Borotra the most lithe and supple tennis player in the world, and the best I could get out of him was an impossibly stiff and wooden swing! But not having had all my natural optimism trodden out of me, I hoped that this case might turn out better and it did.

If a pupil shows any signs of life, after two or three lessons I ask him to give me his impressions of the golf movement. I did so with this lady and she gave a most interesting reply. She said she visualized the movement as "a vertical pillar with a number of circles around it." That showed enterprise and imagination, so I asked what the upright pillar represented. "Activity," she answered promptly. "But," she added, "the circles do not seem to represent passivity."

The main thing wrong with her swing when she came to me was the common fault of throwing her right hip to the right on the way back and then to the left on the way through. I explained this and showed her how she had tried to compensate for this movement by flattening the arcs of her hands and club so as to still come down inside.

"You tell me," she said, "that the pivot has two vital functions, to guide the club head and to generate power. Now I am very interested in the respective spheres of activity and passivity in movement. It is clear that the generating of power is *active*, but am I to assume that the guiding of the club head is *passive*?"

"You are," said I.

"So!" she said. "But may we first make sure we mean

As a Dancer Sees It

the same things by the use of the words 'active' and 'passive'?"

"An excellent precaution," said I, and being always one to learn, I added, "I suggest you lead off and tell me your impressions."

She thought a little and then said, "Well, I am passive when I abstain altogether from acting when I might act."

"You have quoted my dictionary," I remarked.

"Probably," she said. "Indeed, certainly, if we have the same dictionary, as I live in and out of mine—we teachers have to! But if I have understood your analysis of the swing, you mean that that part of it which does not actively resist is purely passive?"

"Quite right," say I. "It should be. The shoulders, arms, wrists, and hands are all *passive* parts in the golf swing; the feet, calves, and buttocks are *active* parts."

"What about the hips? Are they active?"

"They are, but not prominently."

"In a subdued manner," she suggested.

"Yes that is right."

"Then," she said, "activity ends at the hips and passivity begins at the waist. That is good, for, since we have no bones in the waist except for the vertebræ, there is nothing to prevent it being a perfectly passive muscular spiral about which we can turn. Can I think of my waist as being made of strong elastic?"

"What makes you suggest elastic?" I asked. "Most people say steel."

On Learning Golf

"Well, steel in the body would feel like stays and restrict our twist, while elastic allows twist to take place and yet suggests great reactive strength. You tell me that the waist must be flexible not rigid, yet must impose its strength upon the passive part of the swing. I deduce from that, that the good golfer must be strong around the waist line."

"I will not dispute it," said I, "though some good golfers who are touchy about their figures may!"

"Now you tell me," she said, "that your shoulders, arms, and wrists are passive. How far do you go with this idea of passivity? Do you mean that you hit the ball passively?"

"I do," said I. And then, as I saw her eyebrows raised and a protest coming I hastened to add, "The greatest trial of *all* golfers is to retard the club head through the ball. And why is this difficult? Simply because they become active with their hands. Personally I almost never strike the ball too soon because I am, by instinct and training, a passive golfer.

"That," I added, "is why I am a good golfer. Golf is a *passive* game; its dominating sensation is passivity. That accounts for the curious fact that the worse I feel, the better I play! When I am fine and fit, I am active and apt to be a bad golfer, but after a night out I am a bit subdued—and usually very, very good."

"Do you mean that seriously?" she asked.

"Of course I do. And it's not a freak idea, it is a profound golfing truth. Think of all the golfing maxims

As a Dancer Sees It

which have come down the years to us. 'Slow back,' 'Don't press,' 'Follow through,' 'Take it easy,' 'Let your club head do the work'—not one of them enjoining *activity*. I repeat, golf is a *passive* game."

"Is it difficult to get excitable people to be passive?" she asked, going off at a tangent.

"It is," said I. "But it is worth it, because many times when I have cured a nervous pupil's golf nerves, it has helped their general nervous condition enormously. In fact, a good golf lesson is better for the nerves than bromide *or* a month in the country!

"But let's come back to your lesson," I suggested. "What part of the swing do you find it most difficult to keep passive?"

"I think the shoulders," she answered. "I either want to resist or to help with them, and I can't quite make out which it is. I know they feel they want to stiffen, while you tell me they should keep loose. For a long time I have been able to keep my hands passive; it was only recently that I found I was resisting with my shoulders, and, since I discovered that, I *have* been able to bring the club head down inside."

"Yes. You see, when you loosened your shoulders, you were able to use the elasticity of your waist, which you could not do with your shoulders held stiff. When our right shoulder pushes forward on the return swing, it is because our waist has stiffened up in conjunction with our shoulders. Relax our shoulders and we can immediately use our waist twist again."

On Learning Golf

"Yes I can see that. If I tighten my shoulders I immediately lose the feel of torsion at the waist."

"Again," I said, "if your shoulders and waist lose their flexible passivity, you can no longer *retard* your shoulders so that they will follow down, bringing the club head."

Her eyebrows went up again at that! "But you don't mean to say that I should or *can* retard my shoulders, do you?" she asked.

"Oh yes you can, and what is more, you *must*. The elastic waist and the consequent retarded shoulders have as much to do with the 'flailing' action as has the breaking back of the wrists. One is the counterpart of the other; it is the *whole action* that constitutes the flail."

"I see that. But you are always insisting on the upward stretch. How can I stretch up through the body without actively lifting my shoulders?"

"You must stretch up with legs and hips, and then the shoulders will *come up* passively. Try it and you will see. When you try deliberately and directly to raise your shoulders, you commit one of golf's gravest faults. Keeping the shoulders up must be a *reactive* movement, reactive to the brace of the body. And now that we have cleared the ground a bit, let us return to your image of the upright pillar and the circles. The upright pillar stands for our 'power-stretch,' I suppose."

"Yes that is it."

As a Dancer Sees It

"And the circles?"

"Well, they give us a sense of never moving any member of our body except *around* the pillar. But they also convey to me a sense of continuity in movement. Circles are continuous lines and represent the unbroken continuity of the whole movement. Also, what you good players do not seem to realize is that you make your movements *one after another*, never altogether. That gives me the image of a set of spirals moving progressively upward right out to the club head."

"Yes?" said I, interested.

"Yes. And I think it is this connecting together in progression that makes the golf feel so difficult to acquire. I feel it as a force which comes out of the ground, gets into my feet, climbs up my legs and hips, passes on through shoulders and arms, and so to the club head. Only, by the time I feel it has reached the club head, the club head is a couple of feet past the ball. *That* is what I mean by continuity."

"Oh is it!" I gasped and then when I got my second wind, "But that sounds to me less like *continuity* than *acceleration*."

"Maybe," she said. "But if it is a gathering up of power, it is essentially a continuous gathering up. Each feel in the whole movement is joined in unison to the forthcoming one—*anticipating* it one might say."

"But do you suggest that the feel precedes the movement?" I asked.

On Learning Golf

"Of course I do. You know it does. You told me to prepare my feel as I walked to the tee, as I waggled. What is that but anticipation? You fellows excel because you anticipate. You know the correct feels and their correct succession, and you step up to a ball conscious and confident of what will happen. So there is nothing to hamper your swing, no hesitation and no hurry; the anticipation has established the correct continuous feels in you."

"How did you come to know that?" I asked, conscious that she was perfectly correct.

"Well," she smiled, "you may remember that I not only dance, I teach and therefore analyze dancing. Dancing is movement, and movement is life; so you must not be surprised if my analyzing has gone beyond my own sphere and trespassed into yours! And I *was* right, wasn't I?"

CHAPTER XVIII

Power

o

MOST of us do not pay enough attention to what we are told, *how* we are told it, or by whom we are told it. In fact most of us need to learn how to learn. When I use the words "power," "strength," "energy," or even "moving force," some of my pupils take no notice whatever—they do not try to understand or analyze what I mean.

Some pupils of course do try to understand, and they soon realize the difference between the expressions which I have so carefully selected to indicate *power* and those which they had previously confused with them, such as "speed," "quickness," "velocity," and even "hurry." Which distinction is highly desirable, because, if they aim at speed, quickness, velocity, and hurry, they will kill any chance they may have of swinging with strength.

It is the *strength* of the swing of a very good player that intrigues us. He seems to swing slowly, even lazily, yet drives prodigious distances, and we marvel at it and wonder why we cannot do the same. For me there is nothing to wonder at; he swings strongly from his legs upwards while we swing quickly from the club head downwards by means of our shoulders,

On Learning Golf

arms, and hands. He tries to produce power in his swing; we try to impart speed to the club head.

And please remember before we go on to consider its application that power at golf is centered around the hips. Please note *centered around;* the power is not *produced* by the hips (or very little of it is) but by the feet, calves, and thighs—but it is gathered up and given the correct centrifugal golf direction by the hip brace and pivot. And we will fail to drive the ball far and straight as soon as we fail *to take control of the club from the top of the swing with the feet, calves, and thighs.*

Now each shot in golf is a separate situation, and when we contemplate a situation—preparatory to playing the shot—we have to sense through our carefully built-up sense of feel how much power we need. How much *power,* not how much *swing.* A half-shot with a mashie does not mean a half-swing with that club but a swing with half power. We can play—or we should be able to play—a three-quarter shot with a full swing or a full shot with a three-quarter swing. I realize that this conception may be difficult to grasp, but it lies at the root of the superiority of the really great golfer.

I say the *really great* golfer because there are many well-known and successful players who can play nothing but full shots; a *controlled* shot is right outside their golfing range. Yet the great golfer plays every shot controlled, that is he plays every shot with what

Power

he feels to be the correct degree of power *not* at full pressure. This *control* is the secret of his greatness.

The test of a golfer's control is in his ability to play a shot of 70 yards *with every iron club in his bag.* Think that out; it will give you an idea of what control of power means. Every shot will be played *firmly,* but the power applied will obviously have to be varied greatly with the different clubs.

I do not claim that I was ever a great player but I did teach myself to perform this *tour de force,* for a *tour de force* it is. It took me most of my golfing life to learn how to do it. "And why," you may ask, "should you expect us ordinary golfers to be able to do a thing which it took you, an expert, a lifetime to learn?" Well, I did not say I expected you to be able to do it . . . what I do say is that understanding how it is done and *endeavoring* to do it yourself will give you a real conception of controlled power in the golf swing.

In my opinion, we cannot lay too much stress upon this matter of *getting the right conceptions.* It is surprising what you can get people to do once they clearly understand what it is that has to be done. To reverse this, I contend that many of us are playing bad golf not because we are incapable of playing good golf but simply because we are thinking of golf in the wrong way.

I have known cases of such players who improved their swings and their games *without intending to,* simply because they came across and adopted a better

On Learning Golf

conception of the swing. The truth is, of course, that just as if we appreciate good manners we will become good mannered in spite of ourselves; so also, if we appreciate the true ethics of the golf strokes, we will become good golfers.

Why do I use the word "ethics"? Well, because golf *is* a matter of ethics, that is (according to my dictionary) "relating to manners or morals." To prove this, cast your eye round the club room. The chances are you will find the most modest man in the club is also the best player *and* that he is out in the caddie shed. I have never known a great golfer who was not modest, and that goes for Walter Hagen, who in spite of his showmanship was a charmingly modest fellow and a great gentleman.

I hope that the reason why I have wandered off into moral implications in this particular chapter is clear. Our subject is power and power like fire is a good servant but a bad master. Uncontrolled power is the very devil—in golf or anywhere else.

In golf, power must be controlled in two ways: in the matter of *morals* and in the matter of *mechanics*. The mechanical control we may liken to the control of a motor car. The power at golf—the gasoline—is represented by the nails in our shoes, no gasoline, no power! But this power is not applied direct; it works through a clutch, and the clutch in the golfer's mechanism is the hips. That is where the power is gathered up, given its right direction, and put into action or not. Then the

Power

hands we can compare with spark plugs—get them operating too soon or too late in the cycle of operations and your swing backfires. Your swing like the ignition on your car must be *timed*.

Without suggesting that this comparison should be pressed too far, it has its value. One of the points it emphasizes is that clutch slip must be guarded against—that is, there must be no slip, no sloppy movement in your hip work.

We must be fully conscious of how our hips should operate. If the right hip twists inwards as the hips return on the forward swing, we will have swung *from in-to-out*—that is, correctly. But if the right hip is allowed to slip outwards and around on the downward swing, this result cannot be achieved. This is because the club head performs the same actions as does the right hip; they are connected (as regards direction) by the right shoulder.

The effect of bringing our right hip inwards with a twisting movement is to guide the right shoulder in the way it should go. The right shoulder is totally subjective to the right hip; so, when the latter is braced and twisted *inwards*, the shoulder follows, coming inside and behind the ball—*in-to-out*.

Do not think that all this is a digression from our subject, power. For power must be guided as well as produced. We find that it is comparatively easy to drive the ball far; the difficulties begin when we want to add "and straight"; that is when we want our power

On Learning Golf

applied with great accuracy. And in this matter of the accurate application of power, hip brace and movement are fundamentally vital.

Now this twisting inwards movement of the hips demands a muscular effort from the legs which is worth analyzing. As we pivot back, we *turn,* whereas on the forward swing, we *twist.* That is true even though a certain amount of muscular effort *is* needed to pivot back. Considering the swing as a whole, we have to gather up and increase our power gradually. The movement that starts up as a gentle turn develops on the down swing into a fierce twist. The turn is preparatory to the twist. So the effort of the leg muscles begins to be felt at the end of the backward pivot and is felt increasingly until the climax of the follow-through is reached.

The inward twist of the hips as we come down and through the ball demands great muscular activity in the calves and thighs, the generators of power in the golf swing, and it is the controlled direction of the hips that sees to it that this power is smoothly and gradually applied in the exactly correct direction. So we must incorporate into our swing a hip movement which we can recognize and control by a definite *feel,* so that by *feel* we may control the degree and direction of power in our swings.

So "turn and then twist" must be our slogan. These are the *basic* feels of the golf swing; other feels which we may add to them may help us in building up *repeatability,* but they will only hinder if we have not built upon "turn and then twist" as our fundamental basis.

There is more power in the golf swing than that which comes from the legs; much of it comes from the flexibility of the body. "Flexibility" is different from "flail" yet it has similar reactions in our swing. A man of twenty-eight will be less flexible than he was at eighteen and more flexible than he will be at thirty-eight, but at eighteen it might be a *loose* flexibility, at twenty-eight a *free* flexibility, and at thirty-eight a *controlled* flexibility. Every shade and inflection of flexibility adds to or takes from our power.

A man who can only move his shoulders in conjunction with his hips has little chance of becoming a golfer. He is stiff and wooden. We must be able to "leave our shoulders behind." They have no direct torsional connection with the hips and must be able to rotate while the hips are held firm and unmoving by the brace. The fact that our whole body produces torque is what gives power to our swing, and, as we delay our shoulders, we add to the power. On the other hand, if we contract our shoulder muscles in an endeavor to give power to the blow (to "hit harder"), we produce the opposite effect. The shoulder and back muscles must be flexible so that the torque of the body can be picked up by the shoulders and flung into the club head.

The shoulders are midway between the two ex-

On Learning Golf

tremes of the swing, our feet and the club head, and their function like that of the arms and hands is *passive;* they *must* be passive to pass along the power generated by the body. While your shoulders are passive, your swing will be powerful and *alive;* the moment you tighten your shoulder muscles and try to *hit* with them, your swing becomes dead.

This is very important; so let us look at it in another way also. One of the most difficult faults to cure in golf is that of the right shoulder coming forward and *outside* on the way down. It should come down *inside* and, when it does not, it is because it *has become part of the hips;* its connection with the hips is so lacking in flexibility that it is controlled by them and follows their movement. Actually we should use the flexibility of our back muscles to *delay* our shoulder action (in its relation to the pivot) in the same way that we allow our wrists to break back in order to set up delay in our club head.

It is not sufficient to delay the club head through the flexibility of the wrists only; shoulder flexibility must be added. When our right shoulder persists in coming forward, it is because this flexibility has been lost by the muscles of the back being *too tense.*

Now I have already told you that the club head follows the movement of the right hip; that is, the brace forward and to the left of the right hip will induce the swing that feels to go from in-to-out. How does the right shoulder operate in this?

Power

When you study the *feel* of flexible shoulder action, you will find a number of sensations. One curious sensation is that we do not feel that the right shoulder comes *inside* from the front of our body but from behind it. We feel not that it is being *pulled* inside by the muscles of the chest, but that it is being *pushed* inside by the muscles of the back. I talked of this feeling to a well-known surgeon and he told me that it was indeed a correct interpretation of the anatomical facts. The muscles which hold us together and yet allow us flexibility are the cross muscles which join the base of the back (at the waist) to the shoulders. He also explained that unless these muscles are held, as we feel it, very loosely, the shoulders have no choice but to move reactively with the waist—which is in fact what we want them to do in nearly every human activity *except golf!*

Here is a little test of your own flexibility. Stand with your feet together facing the wall and close to it. Without moving your feet turn half right (so that you are looking square at the wall on your right). You can do this easily because you can turn (*a*) from the knees, (*b*) from the waist, and (*c*) from the neck; probably you will use each of the three. Now turn farther, looking into the corner which is three-quarters behind you. Then farther still, looking directly behind you. How far can you go? At the farthest stretch, you will feel coming into play the muscles which come into play at the top of your swing. Then, if you start again and this

On Learning Golf

time turn *left,* you will feel the corresponding muscles which come into action as you finish forward.

You can get some interesting and quite useful *feels* from that little experiment. The point to watch is that, though the back muscles (those I have been describing) will be felt to *stretch* and so to come into action at the extremes of our turn in either direction, *they must not be held tight.* If they are held tight, shoulder flexibility is destroyed—just as wrist flexibility is destroyed by tightening the hand muscles and with just as fatal an effect upon the "flail." For the flail comes from the combined flexibility of all the muscles above the waist.

Now I know that I have been lecturing on the pivot and flexibility and that this is a chapter on power. But I know also that undirected power is no use in golf, and it is the function of the pivot to gather up power from its main sources (which are below the waist) and redirect it so that it emerges from the club head as centrifugal *swing.*

We gather up power through our physical make-up, but the gathering up and redirecting has to be guided by our sense of *feel.* The instant that sense of feel is lost or becomes disconnected, our swing becomes disconnected also—and our power evaporates into thin air, like the sparkle from champagne when the cork is left out!

CHAPTER XIX

Interlude for Instruction

o

A MATHEMATICIAN EXPLAINS

THIS is another true story that will show you what an interesting variety of people I meet and how many and different ways there are of thinking about golf.

One day a player walked into my shop and inquired for me. I happened to be out, but he booked a lesson for the following day. He was an internationally famous mathematician and scientist and by no means of the abstract unpractical type.

"Do you know anything about mathematics?" he asked as we walked over to the practice ground.

If I had not known who he was, I might have dropped into the trap but, "Not a figure!" says I.

"But they told me you had been a schoolmaster," he said, "and that you had a leaning towards the scientific, especially in golf."

"That is true. But I was a pretty poor schoolmaster, and what even the good ones know about mathematics is no use in golf. You can't work out the golf swing in graphs, you know."

"Oh, who told you you could not?"

"No one told me, but what I know about graphs does not seem to bear any more relationship to golf than

On Learning Golf

does—let us say the green grass on the fairway here to the Eiffel Tower, which you can see away in the distance yonder."

"*Green* grass!"—he laughed ironically. "Who told you it is green? And is it?"

"Oh I don't know! Anyway I thought you had come out here to have a golf lesson, not to plumb the depths of my ignorance."

"Do you know anything about Einstein?" he asked completely undisturbed.

"If by Einstein you mean his theory," said I getting one back on him, "of course I know nothing about it. At least, all I *do* know is that only twelve people in the world are said to understand it and you're one of them."

"Actually you probably know quite a lot about it," he said, "only you cannot express it in simple language."

"Well no more can you," said I briefly. "For if you could, many more people would understand it."

"Let us see! Firstly you must realize that golf is a four-dimensional game . . . *time* of course being the fourth."

"That is a good one," said I. "What are the other three?"

"Well, I am coming to that. Will you please play me a shot or two?"

We had a caddie out to scout the balls, and there was another watching from out to the right of us. I

A Mathematician Explains

took a few preliminary swings and then hit a very sweet shot off the turf with my brassie, clean and long with just a little pull at the end.

"Now," he said, "what did you see?"

"Well," said I, "I did not lift my head too soon, so I did not see the ball rise. I saw it in the air and then saw it carry a bit to the left as it dropped."

"Good. Now what did the caddie see? *He* saw the ball come out of the sky too, but he saw it drop to the right. And the fellow out in the wood there saw a simple rise and fall without deviation. So you see that you three fellows would all have described the same operation quite differently; all the descriptions might have been accurate—yet they would (on the surface) have described different flights. That is relativity."

"But what has that to do with golf?"

"Nothing perhaps, except to warn you against hasty conclusions—even when you see things with your own eyes. So do not be too sure the grass is green!"

"Oh drat you and your green grass! What do I care if it is green or blue or black. . . ."

"I knew a painter who said it *was* black," he said.

"Drat him too," said I. "You are getting me hot and bothered. What about this lesson you came out to have?"

"I am having it," he said. "In my own way. I am getting my mind right for the real work, when it comes."

"By which time," said I, "I'll probably be a raving

On Learning Golf

lunatic. And don't ask me how I know I am not one now. I *do* know the answer to that one!"

"Oh! Do you?" he said quizzically. "But tell me this: how many dimensions do you swing your club head through?"

After a pause, to scratch my head I suggested, "Two, I should think. Up and down."

"Not so bad! You are only a third out. You said 'Up' and 'down' but your club also goes 'around.'"

"Well, around is not a dimension."

"Oh, isn't it! Don't you tell your pupils to swing wide?"

"Yes I do. I tell them to take the club head back wide and throw it out in the widest arc they can—that is what I call width."

"Well, that is better than nothing. But do your pupils all understand it that way? I did not."

"I can't help what you do not understand."

"But you should. You are paid by me to make me understand."

"Yes, I know. But have you heard the character sketch—one Englishman a damned fool, two Englishmen a club, three Englishmen a great Empire? Well, I am just one Englishman!"

"Yes, I guessed that early on. But I am trying to understand the swing my way. The trouble with you Pros is that you only understand the swing your way; so you want us to understand it your way too. That is why you are really very little use to anyone except

A Mathematician Explains

people of low intellectual grade. They do not understand anything anyhow so it does not matter what you tell them. Those who become good learn by imitation, those who do not work things out in their own minds—which is fatal because they have nothing to think with."

"I don't entirely agree with that. They *are* difficult to teach, but so are you!"

"Exactly! But in my case that is your own fault. You do not know enough about golf to make me understand it my way. They told me you were a scientific teacher . . . rubbish! You tell me to 'swing through an inclined plane'—that is where people get the idea you are scientific. You are just an advanced slogan-monger. Telling the best girl of some wealthy gent to swing through an inclined plane! What does she know of inclined planes?"

"You're asking me!" said I.

"You do not swing through an inclined plane," he said. "You swing through a vertical plane but with *depth*."

"Well, perhaps you are right. But how the hell can I tell a man to swing deep? When he thinks of depths, he thinks of Australia and bunkers and his grave. You can't have depth sideways."

"Oh can't you? How do you know you can't?"

"But what about the golf lesson you wanted?"

"I am having it and it is going very nicely. Only negatively!"

On Learning Golf

"Negatively?"

"Yes."

"But you can't learn negatively."

"Oh can't you!" he said. "Which impresses you most: $2+2=4$ or $2+1=4$?"

"Yes, I see that. I know which is right; so $2+1=4$ impresses me because of its contradiction to the truth."

"So the *negative* impresses you the more. Now! You tell me that to make the ball *roll* is the greatest art of the golfer."

"Yes I do."

"You also say that to make the ball roll you must put 'top-spin' on it."

"Agreed."

"Well that, I must point out, is a negative also because no one *can* put top-spin on a golf ball."

"Oh no! You want me to believe that when I putt a ball all along the ground, and it runs and runs and runs, rolling over and over and over, I have not put top-spin on it?"

"You have not put the fraction of a particle of top-spin on it."

"But I can make the ball roll and you can't. Why is that then?"

"Because with your skill and experience you can make your club head 90° vertical and can pass it over the ground to connect with the ball square to its horizontal axis. Then as the bottom of the ball is stuck to the ground by the friction set up by gravity and the

A Mathematician Explains

top is free to move, the top moves first and you set up your over and over movement. Just as if your feet suddenly stuck in the ground as you were running, you would fall flat on your face."

"But you are not going to tell me that I can't impart what I call top-spin in different degrees and so make one ball run more than another. Watch this . . . and this . . . and this . . . ," I said, playing various shots.

"Yes, very skilfully done. But all you have done is to put *less* back-spin on some shots than on others. That is what I meant when I said 'top-spin' in golf is a negative. The only spin you can put on a golf ball is back-spin. To put on top-spin is a physical impossibility—as you will see if you think out where and at what angle the ball would have to be struck to impart it."

"Well, what does it matter to me what sort of spin you call it, so long as I can produce the effect I want?"

"As a player, it does not matter to you at all. The skill with which you can control spin makes you an outstanding player, no matter what you call it. But as a teacher, it does matter to you because the fact that you call things by their wrong names prevents me learning from you. Your teaching capacity is negative."

"Thank you," said I. "Fortunately there are plenty of people who do not agree with you. And anyway if that is so, why are you taking this lesson?"

"I love talking to simple people."

"Hell! Do you know that I have beaten Henry Cotton—and anyone who can do that is not so simple!"

On Learning Golf

"It is because you play golf in the simple way that you beat him! Experience has taught you the easiest way of playing. By dint of that experience and unceasing practice, you have learned to draw a straight line in the most simple way."

"A straight line?"

"What is a straight drive but a straight line?—a long one and drawn without a ruler too! Also it is in four dimensions. Yet you are simple enough to wonder why people cannot play golf—and why you cannot teach them."

"Put like that it does sound complex. But now I come to think of it, I play golf in one dimension only—straight ahead."

"And what about **time**?"

"I ignore it!—I play in **one dimension only**—straight ahead."

"Like a worm crawling straight to its hole?"

"Yes, exactly, except in my figure!"

"You mean to tell me that you only try to knock the ball along the ground?"

"Yes."

"When you play high shots over trees? When you deliberately put on *back-spin*, do you conceive all that as golf in one dimension?"

"I do."

"Well, why didn't you tell me that before? Here we have been troubling ourselves with Einstein, only to find now that you play in one dimension only."

A Mathematician Explains

"Well, it's a reasonable simplification, isn't it?"

"Possibly so; it is if you mean what I think you do . . . that you play golf in four dimensions with a one-dimensional outlook."

"I don't know about my dimensional outlook; what I try to feel is that I am in a position to play straight along the ground."

"Well, that certainly seems a very simple outlook and in your case it is undeniably effective. Do you think that I will ever be able to play along the ground?"

"Good Lord, no! Only twelve of us can do that *and I am one of 'em.*"

CHAPTER XX

Temperament

THE secret of success in golf lies in temperament and that is true whatever grade of golf you may aspire to play. Tournaments are not always, not even *usually*, won by the greatest stylists. They go to the men with the best balanced outlook on the game. And how frequently we have seen the fellow with a rank, bad swing take the half-crown off a man who looked far better on the tee.

Do not mistake me. It is an excellent thing to be a stylist, if your style is supported and molded by a good golfing temperament. Harry Vardon before the Great War and Bobby Jones in the years that followed it were perfect stylists, but they were also perfectly balanced in the psychophysical sense and won more tournaments than any other golfers. On the other hand, Taylor and Braid, who were never deemed stylists at all, almost equaled these two in collecting championships because they were *temperamentally* in the championship class. But you will not find any golfer who is temperamentally weak or unreliable habitually winning big events, however brilliant a stylist he may be.

I suppose we might say that a man's style at golf is evolved from the reactions on one another of his tem-

Temperament

perament and his physical make-up. We may all learn to write from the same copy-book but we will grow up to sign our checks differently, and, though I have been teaching golf for thirty-five years now, I have yet to find two people who play alike. No matter how much you tried to teach two people to play alike, the results would be surprisingly different.

We do not all play golf for the same reason, of course, and that may affect the way we play it. Some of us play it for a living. Many play it on doctor's order and more still for exercise! There are more individual reasons too, and I have come across some odd ones in my time. A lady came to me once with her child, a girl of about fourteen. She said, "I am not going to make my daughter an intellectual; I want you to make her a golf champion." "I'll do my best," said I. "But why do you want her to be a golf champion?" "Oh," she said, "look at . . . and . . . and . . . ," and rattled off the names of champions who had made fine marriages! That was the idea, and I may tell you that in due course it proved successful.

Sometimes, of course, we forget *why* we took up golf, and the game or some aspect of it runs away with us. That is the way fanatics are born.

I remember one old fellow who sent his valet round to get me out of bed at one o'clock in the morning because he had something to tell me that could not wait. When I got to the old chap's place, there he was in the garden, swinging away like mad by the light of a lan-

On Learning Golf

tern hung on a tree. There was a table with glasses on it and a bottle of whiskey, and, while I recompensed myself for being turned out, he explained to me that he had just discovered the secret of golf! He had his two elbows tied across his chest with a double strand of Sandow elastic which kept them, and especially kept the right one, from *lifting* at the top of the swing.

Well, I had just about forgiven him that one when he again sent for me in the middle of the night. I toddled down because he was amusing and really not a bad old chap. Well, there he was in the garden again, swinging away in his pajamas. This time he had a piece of elastic pinned to his coat between his shoulder blades; he pulled it over his right shoulder and held it between his teeth. He said it prevented him looking up, which I believed, and that it was the secret of good golf, which I did not.

Of course, the tricks did not work because he could not tie himself up with elastic out on the course, and, having got used to swinging with it, he naturally went to bits when he took it off. He would have done much better if he had used his imagination instead of elastic. But that happened to be how he got his fun out of golf!

So as you see, golf is not the same thing to all men; and according to the way we look at the game, so will our ambitions be formed and the temperament in which we approach it be developed.

If a fellow is content to be able to knock the ball one hundred and fifty yards down the fairway, there

Temperament

is no point in explaining the flail to him—he would not be interested. Comparatively few people *are* interested in playing the game as well as they could play it. In particular, most youngsters think of nothing but hitting their tee shots "miles" and do not seem to mind missing 80 per cent of their other shots, though as we all know, it is the "other shots" which enable you to go round in a reasonable score. If you can chip and putt decently, you can always get yourself a decent score. I know lots of men who can go round St. Cloud in under 80 and never hit a clean golf shot the whole time.

Now these matters of what one wants to do in golf and how one wants to do it are directly related to temperament, but let me get right back to the heart of the subject by telling you a story which is about temperament and nothing but!

It started when a lady came to me for lessons. She did well, so well that one day she said, "Do you know, my game has improved so much that my husband is going to take a course of lessons with you. I'm so sorry." "Why be sorry?" said I. "I'm delighted." She looked at me with a slight smile. "You don't know my hubby," she said. "He is the most violent-tempered man in the world."

Well, in due course he turned up. He looked wild and he *was* wild in the sense that he let his emotions run loose! Being prepared, I naturally took up a meek and mild attitude, which egged him on to more and

On Learning Golf

more furious bursts of temper every time he missed the ball—which incidentally was every time he swung at it! And every time he missed he would fling his driver on the ground and yell to me, "What did I do wrong *that* time?"

I suggested a few things which I knew would not work, and he got wilder still. Then, suddenly after a particularly furious burst of rage, I said to him quietly, "Let me see your driver." He handed it to me ungraciously. "Old friend?" I asked examining it. "Got it at Oban," he growled. I looked him in the eye, shut my lips, took the club in both hands, and broke it in two across my knee—and threw the pieces in a corner of the shed.

He went gray and gray-white and speechless. While he was contemplating the wreckage, I bent down and put another ball on the tee. Then I straightened up and said, "Take your brassie." He went to his bag like a lamb and went on with the lesson much more quietly—which was lucky for him because if he had kept on fuming I would have broken every club in his bag. He is a different man and a very different golfer to-day.

At a later lesson I told him the true story of a golfer who on his first appearance at St. Andrews became so enraged with his putter that he threw it out of bounds at the Elysian fields and tore up his card. Yet the next time he played there he won the Open! But he did not win the Open until he had curbed his temper.

Now these two stories are nearly everyone's. But to

Temperament

get as mad as the proverbial meat-axe because we miss a shot is the sign of a young golfer. The experienced golfer does not get mad when he misses a shot because he knows that if he does so the chances are that he will miss the next one too. And I doubt if it is any more difficult to build up control of your temperament in golf than it is to build up control of your swing *once you appreciate the need*.

But I think we must go back again from this point to the question of *why* you play golf. Because the state of mind and the temperamental strains of (*a*) a tired business man playing purely for relaxation and (*b*) a Pro fighting for a championship on the last green are so immensely different that their problems are different—or at least arise in very different intensities.

Many big business men and men in public life have told me how great a relaxation they found golf to be. Nothing takes your mind so completely off the daily worries as does a round of golf. Each of us, whatever his rating as a golfer may be, has to pay attention to the job in hand; so much attention that for a couple of hours we are in a new world and the problems and tensions of our normal world are forgotten.

During the building up of the Treaty of Versailles, Woodrow Wilson, Lloyd George, Sir Elmsley Carr, and Sir George Riddell used often to come out to the club between sessions. I still have a book which Mr. Wilson left in my shop one day, on the same day in fact that I had a chat with Admiral Beatty and Mr. Boyden,

On Learning Golf

an American lawyer who was in Paris on the same job. I remember seeing Mr. Winston Churchill play once at Barton-on-Sea and I have been told that during his hardest days at Berlin, just before the present war, Sir Nevile Henderson never missed an opportunity of getting in a round—or even a few holes—between those fateful conversations.

Sir George Riddell was the best golfer of those I have mentioned, but men of this eminence rarely make first-class players; they play simply for exercise and relaxation, not always for even pleasure.

Again there are plenty of people, too many in fact, who play purely as a pastime. I say too many because to my mind these are the most devastating of all golf bores. A keen man is always interesting because of his keenness, but to hear a recapitulation of a round which was only played to pass the time—and is only being recapitulated to pass some more time—is the depths beyond which golf boredom cannot sink.

At the other extreme of keenness, you find the American Pros. They will play all day, fill in between rounds with practice, and take you out before breakfast or after dinner to see if you can't give them a few hints! I remember a championship week at Muirfield. We had all played our two qualifying rounds and had an hour's practice and were not sorry to get back to the club house and relax. But in came Lawson Little. "Come on, boys," he said, "come outside and see me hit a few shots." So out we went and sat on a bank to watch

Temperament

him hit literally hundreds of drives—asking questions all the time. That at ten o'clock at night! It keeps light late in Scotland in June.

I wonder if you remember Tom Webster's cartoon of Leo Diegel going out for a little putting practice—with a whole armful of putters to try out. I saw Leo actually do that. It was another championship occasion, and he lost the title on the greens. He had lost his touch and tried to get it back by changing his putter, but the trouble was that he was nervous and jumpy. One has to be very calm and quiet to putt well.

Temperament is pre-eminently important in putting because good putting is so largely a matter of *confidence*. You can only *stroke* the ball when you are quietly confident; otherwise you jerk it. You can always drive or play big shots reasonably well, because that is done more with the grosser muscles, but the finer touch required for putting is a much more delicate matter and so is much more liable to be put out of gear and *jerked* by nervous tension.

Bad putters habitually *stab* the ball: that is why they are bad putters. Good putters jerk the club when they are nervous, which is basically quite a different fault.

My teaching is built up around the principle of *playing by feel*: that is, through our muscular reflexes and controls. This leaves it to our muscles to swing the club and sets us free to give a little attention to our mental state—to inhibit the urge to hurry, and to go quietly

On Learning Golf

and methodically about the job. We know that when we are in a quiet state we can play the shot as well as we know how; therefore if we can *make* ourselves quiet and relaxed, we will allow our muscular control system to work.

To illustrate this point let me tell you a little story from my own experience. In 1927 I was runner-up in the Belgian Open at Knocke and won the Dutch Open at The Hague, both in the same week. They were then 36-hole tournaments, and in each I did a 69 in the second round. Now here I should tell you what you may already know, that I was never a first-class golf tournament player for two reasons: I was not physically strong enough, and temperamentally I was too highly strung.

The story is about the last hole I played at The Hague, to complete my 69 and beat Henry Cotton by one stroke. After an indifferent drive from the last tee, the home green seemd to get smaller and smaller—it was triangular in shape with the hole tucked well down in the apex, a clump of trees to the right and a bunker on the left. Henry was playing behind me, and I had a pal standing on the 17th green who signaled to me before I played my second that Henry had got his 4 and we were level over the 35 holes.

I deliberately pushed out all the surge of thoughts and emotions that came rushing into my mind and said to myself, "Now you old fool, *keep quiet* and play this shot as if you were showing a pupil at St. Cloud how it

Temperament

should be played." Well, I got myself quieted down and then played my shot—straight onto the flag but about ten yards short.

Knowing that I was a good putter, I said to myself, "Well, I shall tie anyway." But I did not a bit relish the idea of having to go out and play another 18 holes. But there it was—or rather there *I* was, on the green but ten yards from the hole. So I went through the same back-chat with myself, to get quieted down. Then I putted, a firm, clean *stroking*—and when I *did* look up, it was just in time to see the ball drop into the hole, to win me the title by a single stroke.

Tournaments are mental agony to most Pros, and having had my fill I have never played in another since that day. We all know the horrid feeling that creeps over us as we walk to the first tee—and the sigh of relief when the ball does get away. Then we calm down and are better until the bad luck chips in (as it is apt to do in golf!). *Then* we begin to get annoyed, and that is the worst possible state for a golfer.

What can be done about it? Well, I will tell you a simple little story about a very young pupil of mine, and you can read into it whatever you *can* read into it.

One day I was out on the course amusing, rather than teaching, a little girl of seven. On one occasion she showed a little impatience and I said to her very seriously, "Don't you get angry! Only badly brought-up little girls get angry, and you are a nicely brought-up little girl." I always remember the way she looked at

On Learning Golf

me—sideways, like a little robin. After that she would say to me sometimes, "Am I getting angry?" And I would say, "Well, your ears *do* look a little white; let me feel your pulse," or I would put my ear to her back to hear if her heart was beating too fast. She took it all so seriously and was intensely pleased when one day I said, "Now that's better; not so angry as last time you did that!" And then one day I told her she was quite cured (which she was) and she was in ecstasies!

All very childish if you like. But those lessons in golf psychology stood her in good stead. She grew up to be a champion and her manners on the course were always a pleasure to see and a pattern to be followed.

If you wish to hide your character, do not play golf. It will be revealed on the course. I was telling this one day to a very irascible chap, and he said, "Well, what would you do about it, if you were me?" I replied quietly, "Ride a bicycle."

Of course, it is not only golfers who are afflicted this way. I was telling these stories one day to my little girl, who though only eleven is an ardent pianist, and she told me the following tale of Schubert. One day Schubert was composing at the piano, and he became annoyed with the little finger of his left hand—because it would not articulate properly and so hindered the flow of his thoughts. He became furious with it and wrenched it back with such violence (as if to show the refractory finger how far it *should* articulate) that he

Temperament

dislocated it. And ever afterwards, so the story goes, he was a finger short when he wished to play.

When we come to bedrock, what do we mean when we say that a man has a "good golfing temperament"? We mean that he has sufficient control of himself to produce his best shots *whatever the circumstances may be*. The man who has this starts with a greater advantage than the man with the ideal golfing physique or the man with the fine natural style.

Can you acquire the golf temperament? You certainly can, as I had to do to a considerable degree. And you have got one very great help which I lacked in my novitiate—the idea of learning golf by *feel*. For one of the main advantages of this method is just that it *can* make your game storm-proof, can make you capable of producing your best shots when you need them, irrespective of your state of mind and the condition of the game.

CHAPTER XXI

Interlude for Instruction

o

LARGELY CONCERNED WITH THE WAGGLE

THE most difficult lessons to give are those to players with handicaps around 5 and 6. They are in the "near scratch" class, and when they come to us it is either because they realize they have come to a full stop or because they have struck a thoroughly bad patch which they cannot get themselves out of.

The attitude of these players is very rarely that there is anything wrong with their game. Oh no! It is just that they miss an odd drive or two which puts them in the rough; two or three times in a round their iron shots miss the green, and then maybe a couple of putts that should go down don't, and that (they figure out in the smoke room) is why they are not scratch.

I always start off by telling these people that you have to be a very good golfer to be scratch. Talent and skill are not enough to get you there; your golf must be built on the right foundations.

The trouble with many 5 and 6 handicap men is that they have become as good as their conception of the game enables them to be. Because their swing has not been developed about the correct centrifugal principle, it is *unreliable,* and they have to depend upon a tip being given or an idea coming to them just when

Largely Concerned with the Waggle

they need it. This is a dangerous state of affairs, and the natural result of trying to learn golf by trial and error—that is by trying one thing one day and another the next—with no basic principle to back it up. It is true that that is the way most of us Pros learned, but it takes immense perseverance and a long time!

Well, one day I had one of these 5 handicap fellows come to me for help. I made him hit a ball or two, and he asked me what I thought of his swing.

"Very good indeed," said I. "But you waggle badly. That is all there is wrong with your golf."

"Oh!" said he, a little astonished and more than a little disappointed.

You see he neither expected nor liked what I told him. Because of my reputation as a teacher, he thought that I would have a "cure" for his trouble, and I had none.

I still have no cure for it. Any pupil of mine can cure himself as well as I can cure him by referring back to first principles. If one of my pupils comes to me as to a doctor, not as to a teacher, I just run over the ground work with him, just to make sure he is setting his mechanics in motion properly, and, when we have done this, it is quite easy to put our finger on the trouble.

But to come back to the lesson. This pupil had a particularly fiery waggle, so fiery that its violence threw too much action into his hands which remained active throughout his swing and so made him a *direct hitter*.

On Learning Golf

I explained this to him and continued, "The essence of rhythmic swinging is to be smooth, for only the smooth swing *can* be rhythmic. But if you get undue club head agitation into your preparatory movement (which is what the waggle is) you will get all the feel in your hands, arms, and shoulders, *not* in your legs, hips, and back, which is where you *should* feel that you swing from."

"But I don't see why I can't feel my back and legs when I waggle my way?"

"Well, to put it as briefly as possible, when you waggle your way, the club head sets up movement to which the body must react. The club head is pulling the body; the tail is wagging the dog. It should be the other way round: you need to be subdued and waiting for the action of the body to set up club head movement."

"I see that."

"That is why the preparatory movement of the good golfer is smooth and tiny and controlled. I remember once taking a pupil of mine to see Henry Cotton play, and he noticed the beautiful way Henry prepared his swing. As he said, 'You feel as he looks down the fairway that he already has the sense of how he is about to perform—you can see him feeling the club head through his pivot.' Now that was a shrewd analysis, and I was interested to hear what my pupil would say about Henry's methods on the green. His comment was, 'Not much preparation there!' 'No,' said I, 'he

Largely Concerned with the Waggle

does not putt as he drives. If he did, we would see the finest scoring machine yet known in golf.'"

"Yes, that is interesting. But tell me, if I must not waggle my club with my hands—what *may* I do with them?"

"As nearly as possible—nothing," said I. "The hands are not direct agents in producing the power of a golf shot; they are a *connection* between the lower part of the body (where the power comes from) and the club head, and they must remain nothing more than a connection. If you *use* your hands, consciously or not, you break connection."

"Must a good swing be 'connected'?"

"Indeed it must. The great player is great because his swing is connected and therefore reliable. He makes an indifferent shot only when he does lose connection. The reason why he uses only a three-quarter swing is because that is as far back as he can go without the risk of breaking the connection."

"Exactly what do you mean by 'breaking connection'?"

"Here is a gross example. If I intentionally 'open' my hands at the top of the swing, I lose connection and have to put in compensatory movements on the way down, to try to correct the results of the error—which they cannot fully do. The result is unreliable and at its best unsatisfactory."

"Is a 'connected' swing the same thing as a 'compact' one?"

On Learning Golf

"Yes. How would you define a compact swing?"

"Well, a swing which seems to be working as one, without loose parts and yet free to work."

"Good. That will do for a 'connected' one too. And I assure you again that you will never develop a compact and connected swing as long as you waggle so fiercely."

"But my swing cannot be so bad. I'm 5 handicap and was 2 once."

"I did not say you could not play reasonably effective golf with a disconnected swing. Ninety-nine swings out of every hundred *are* disconnected, but the odd one per cent belong to the scratch and plus men."

"But do you tell me there is all that difference between say a 3 handicap and a plus 3?"

"Indeed I do. I will narrow it down further and say that there is more difference between a plus 3 man and a scratch golfer than there is between a 3 handicap and an 18 handicap man."

"And you seriously think that the main thing which keeps me out of the top class is the use of my hands?"

"I do. I want you to feel your hands only as a connecting link in the whole mechanism, not as a separate working part. Try to play a short chip shot *guiding it and giving it its power entirely from the knees*. When you can do that you will know what it is to feel connected."

"But I cannot bring the club head forward without bringing it forward with my hands."

Largely Concerned with the Waggle

"Yes, you can! And you *must* because until you have learned to do that you will never swing 'connectedly.'"

"But I would be more than satisfied if I could play like R. A. Whitcombe, who says he hits the ball *all with his right hand.*"

"Surely you would! But in my view Whitcombe is confusing an effect with a cause if he ever used that phrase, which I doubt. We know what he *means*. Of course, my best shots all *feel* right-handed too—because the right hand is the one behind the center of force, so it has to do most of the transmitting. But do not confuse *something that happens* with *something which you have to do*. Whitcombe gives you an impression of what happens; I am telling you *how* it happens. And I assure you that if you or Whitcombe or anyone else *tries to hit with the right hand* (or the left or with both for that matter), the shot will be ruined."

"Yes, I see that, and I think you are right about my hands. But I still do not see what my violent waggle has to do with my swing as a whole."

"Well your own phrase suggests the answer to that one! The basic trouble with a violent waggle is that it sets up too intense local reactions and actually *prevents us feeling the swing as a whole*. Always keep in mind that the swing is one and indivisible and must be balanced. If any part of it becomes too active (as it will if you exaggerate any phase of it), the swing is thrown out of balance and you can no longer feel it as

On Learning Golf

a whole. The good golfer rarely loses the feel of the whole; when he does, he makes bad shots like the rest of us."

"Putting it another way," I continued, "any extraneous movement we perform, any *strain* we put on our swing, will push the whole out of shape. There will be a dent where there should be a smooth curve. As soon as we feel the dent we begin to make compensatory movements and before long the rhythm of our swing is completely broken up by the original dent and our subsequent efforts to correct it. The simpler the swing, the better. The ideal is to bring it down to a one point center of feel."

"Why?" he asked.

"Because the correct golf swing is the application of centrifugal force, the center whirling the periphery around. So we must have a firm center for all shots. The shorter the shot, the lower down in our body do we feel the center to be. Fundamentally the whirl around is always the same, but while in the drive we feel we whirl mainly from the hips, in chip shots we feel the whirl comes chiefly from the knees. Actually the power of a golf shot comes *out of the ground* through its resistance to the feet. The hands have nothing to do with it—What sort of a shot could you make if you were suspended with your feet off the ground?"

"Good for you! So . . . ?"

"Well, you begin your swing with a big dent in it—made by your excessive waggle. All through your

Largely Concerned with the Waggle

swing you are trying to straighten that dent out by compensatory movements. When the compensations are coming off, you play to your handicap; when they are not, you don't. And you will never be scratch until you get rid of the dent and so can afford to throw the compensations after it. You see, you will never beat fellows like myself while you have all that extra work to do, all those extra things to go wrong. Sometimes you seem to be playing as well as we do—but it doesn't last! Our art is not to play 9 holes well, but 18 or 36. I call you a 14-hole golfer—which is not a bad rating! I have a 'hole handicap' like that for all my pupils—having no use for the other sort of handicap, the pot-hunter's glory."

"Now I begin to see what you are getting at. I agree that I start my swing jerkily—as you say, with dents in it, and I don't doubt that if I could start more *smoothly* and keep going smoothly right through, I should be able to keep pegging away with a much better average day in and day out. But surely there must be more wrong with my swing than that."

"Perhaps there are some minor mechanical faults; that we cannot know at the moment. You see, you cannot eradicate or work on a minor mechanical fault if you have a *fundamental* fault which impedes you feeling the whole swing. And who knows, when you get your preparatory movements smoother, some of those so-called faulty mechanics may smooth *themselves* out; they may be an *effect* of the strain in your swing.

On Learning Golf

As you know, you do not have to throw *much* sand into a machine to put it out of order."

"So I must begin by waggling smoothly with my pivot, instead of jerkily with my hands. Is that it?"

"Exactly. That is why I use the term 'preparatory movement' instead of waggle when I can. It suggests a quiet diminutive movement of the club head—far removed from violent activity."

"But *can* I change my waggle if I want to? They tell me that Sandy Herd never could."

"True; but Sandy's case was not in the least like yours. He had an excellent, finely responsive waggle or he could not have played the golf he did. All that was troubling him was the abnormal number of times he had to waggle (actually it was fourteen times) before he got his feel settled and could make his shot. It is quite true that he never did succeed in reducing his fourteen to a more normal number. Your trouble is quite different. No matter if you make four waggles, fourteen, or forty, you will *never* get the settled feel that enables you to make a shot with certainty—because your conception of the waggle has been wrong and, far from settling you, yours has *unsettled* you."

"Yes, I see that. And you have given me quite a different idea of it. But now tell me a little more of what you mean by a connected swing, please—or rather how I can *be* connected."

"Well the two extreme points of the golf swing are the *feet* (drawing power from the resistance of the

Largely Concerned with the Waggle

ground) and the *club head* (free to travel through the air). Now if we are to control our swing, there must be an unbroken chain of connections between these two points. One end of the swing is fixed; the other is free but connected; but, if on the way back I (1) open the club face, (2) bend the left arm, (3) relax the right knee, and (4) open the hands—my swing will be completely disconnected. My club head will feel lost."

"Yes."

"If I start a swing in that way, I have to repeat all these breaking-up movements in the reverse way on the way down; otherwise I cannot connect with the ball. 'Some operation' as you may imagine! But if I do none of those things on the way back, if I do *not* open the club face, do *not* bend the left arm, *or* relax the right knee, *or* open the hands, I shall not have to make the corresponding corrections on the way down—and in consequence my swing will become simple and connected instead of complex and disjointed."

"Yes, I see."

"The return movement of the swing starts with the left heel returning to the ground, and this reacts on the legs, hips, pivot, and shoulders to produce the centrifugal sweep of the club head. Every part of the swing reacts naturally and immediately to the rest of it—but, if you introduce breaks and disconnections, this natural certain reaction is lost and the whole swing becomes uncertain."

My pupil took a few swings and drove a couple of

On Learning Golf

balls. "Are those four points you mentioned the only ones where I may lose connection?" he asked.

"No. They are the main points, where the crude breaks occur. As you get those corrected and improve and subtilize your *feel* of the swing, you will discover other and more subtle ones which break the swing up not coarsely but delicately. It is all a question of *degree* of sensibility and control."

"Now look here," my pupil said, hitting more balls down the fairway, "I've taken note of what you said, and yet I have more mistakes in my swing than ever. What do you say about that?"

"I say *fine!* People spend too much time building up swings as per the copybook. A man's swing is largely the result of his conception of what a swing should be, and the best way of correcting a faulty swing is to *get the correct conception.* Now this lesson has altered your conception; so you can recognize faults in your swing that you could not recognize before—apart from probably introducing some new ones!"

"But I want to get better—not worse."

"True. But you came to me because you were at a dead end. You may now go much further back and become really bad, because your swing was full of compensatory movements which will not work now you have a proper conception of what a swing should be. Your choice is plain; you can either:

(1) Go on compensating and remain 5, or
(2) Start working on the new conception."

Largely Concerned with the Waggle

"Well, if I do the latter, what are the chances of real improvement?"

"It's up to you," I said. "I never knew anyone who worked on those lines without making progress. But it means work and it means that at first you must not trouble about results."

"Is it worth it?"

"It is. One day the curtain that has been obscuring your view will be pulled back, and you will play a real golf shot. Then you go on, probably losing that real shot almost as soon as you find it—but never mind. The good shots will recur and become more frequent and just as one day you found you had played a good shot, later you will *play a good hole*. Then it is only a matter of patience and work until 68 appears on your card. Is it worth it? I should say it is!"

CHAPTER XXII

Putting

o

IF you want your golf to be based upon sound principles, beware of the *jeu de mots*. Avoid falling a victim to those slogans and catch-phrases with which golfing talk and golfing writing are so liberally peppered. The slogan is the enemy of thought, and the fact that a phrase has been current around club rooms and courses right through the golfing ages is no guarantee that it enshrines a profound golfing truth—it may be just a superficially bright and catchy phrase. My own view is that the fundamentals of golf are not compressible into slogans.

A large number of these catch-phrases have gathered around putting. We have all heard, "Never up, never in," "A good putter is a match for anyone," and, "Putting is a game within a game," so often that we must be in grave danger of accepting them as true.

I say "grave danger" advisedly. Take "putting is a game within a game." If you accept that and its implication—that putting needs a method of approach and technique different from that of the rest of golf—your chance of ever becoming a first-class putter drops to round about zero. Putting is *not* a game within a game: it is *the* game. It is the essence of correct golfing mech-

Putting

anism. If anyone who has a proper conception of the golf swing will apply this same conception to the putt, his putting will improve in consequence.

Now this chapter is on putting not on catch-phrases, but I want to deal with one more of the latter here because it may help us to get this matter of putting into perspective. "A good putter is a match for anyone." That phrase was popular and accepted as it is now when my great compatriot Harry Vardon was in his prime. Because with the limelight on him Harry had been seen to miss some absurdly short putts, some people (but not the folk he played against) put him down as "a poor putter."

The greatest putter of the time beyond doubt or question was Willy Park. So Willy was pitted against Vardon to confirm the adage that a good putter is a match for anyone. He did not confirm it; how Harry won that match is historic . . . *he pitched so close to the hole that he did not have to putt well.*

So we must rewrite the slogan and make it, "a good golfer is a match for anyone," not a good putter any more than a good driver or a good mashie player. Golf is one whole game. It is true that if you cannot putt you cannot win, for no hole is won until the ball is down—but good scores are only made possible by good play up to the green.

Is it true, you may ask, that, "good putters are born not made," because if so, what is the use of trying to learn how to putt? Another of those wretched catch-

On Learning Golf

phrases you see. You *can* learn to putt. I was born a good putter, but I became an infinitely better one when I learned *how* to putt.

In fact I became so exceptional a putter that after playing the morning round with me at Knocke, Walter Hagen called out to Aubrey across the dining-room, "Your brother is the finest chipper and holer out I have ever seen," and though Walter was an inveterate leg-puller, he *meant* that! I had taken only 29 putts for the round and my holing out up to two yards was exactly one hundred per cent. And oddly enough I had modeled my methods largely upon those of Walter Hagen himself—the King Pippin on the green of his generation and the father of modern golf-green methods. In following his lead I was in good company, even the great Bobby Jones went through a period of "Walter imitation." Though he did not adopt the same wide open stance, he used Walter's reversed overlapping grip and smooth slow follow-through.

To teach yourself to putt successfully, you must study the putt *in its relation to the technique of every other shot in the game,* not as a thing apart. That is why I say to my pupils at the very start of their golfing days, "I putt as I drive."

Of course, having seen with their own eyes the fierce sweeping through of a long drive and mentally compared it with the delicate accuracy with which a short putt is stroked on its way, they look incredulous when I first tell them this. Later, as their understanding of

Putting

the game develops, they see the truth of it—though some of them are then inclined to argue that, "I putt as I drive," should really run "I drive as I putt!"

Now as I have told you, I wanted to find a mechanical action—a golf movement—with which *all* shots could be played, so as to develop perfect and uncomplicated reflex movements. I hope I have already made it clear why it is that if we change our fundamental golf movement for the playing of *any* shot, that shot not only fails to help build up reliable feel and reflex movements—it actually complicates and confuses the feels and reflex movements which have been built up.

Before I had reached my present conclusion on these matters, I knew that Bobby Jones had said that the putting stroke was like any other and that in actual application the Pendulum Stroke is a physical impossibility. Incidentally he had also classified keeping the head still as a fallacious golf maxim. Also one day when Walter Hagen was putting, he turned to Aubrey and said, "I can't stroke from in-to-out to-day."

Now all of this confirmed my opinion that it should be possible to putt as we drive and encouraged me in my search for the method. And you need not be surprised that it took me quite a few years to find and to master it.

Firstly, the fundamental golf movement is centrifugal, and we are used to using centrifugal forces so forcefully that to tone it down until one could stroke home a nasty four-foot putt on a fast green took some

REVERSED OR PUTTING GRIP

POINTS TO STUDY

The reversed overlapping grip gives more right-hand feel. (In fact, the palm of the right hand facing the hole gives the impression that the ball will be "rolled out of the hand towards the hole.")

The club is held not in the tips of the fingers of the right hand, but down at the roots of the fingers. The right thumb is on the top of the shaft.

The right elbow and forearm rest lightly in the curve made by hip and thigh.

The back of the left hand rests lightly on the left thigh. The left elbow is almost facing the hole . . . as is the back of the left hand.

Both knees are slightly bent, the weight is well back on the heels—as if sitting on a shooting stick.

The weight is more on the left foot than on the right. The ball is just inside the left heel.

REVERSED OR PUTTING GRIP

AUBREY

Putting

doing. But when it *was* done, I found I could sink more of these nasty short putts than I could before.

The second big problem I came up against was how to follow through a short putt on a fast green. I took to cutting down my back swing, making it shorter and shorter, but never—it seemed—quite short enough. Then one day while I was practicing on the green, I put my putter down behind the ball and just *rolled* the ball forward—with no back swing at all, only a forward push of the club head from the right hand.

Now I know that this was a foul stroke, but its sensual value to your golfing education cannot be overrated. Try it yourself, and you at once feel and realize how the ball should run off the face of the putter and how little muscular power or pressure is needed to roll the ball into the hole. This muscular power (such as it is) should come entirely through the right hand and forearm; the left only comes into play on the back swing.

Since in putting the movement is so slight and delicate, very little centrifugal force is generated, and it is most difficult to feel the club head; so we try to get as much feel as possible in the right hand. That is the reason for adopting the reverse overlapping grip—it gives increased right-hand feel.

When you first try this trick of rolling the ball towards the hole, you will find that you are holding your right hand and forearm as stiff as a poker. They should not be stiff at all. You should hold your putter

On Learning Golf

no tighter than you hold your pen. In playing the longer shots we mainly need to use the grosser muscles, but we must learn to progressively hold our muscles more and more lightly as the shots become shorter. It is because we do not realize this that we are bad putters, not because we are born to be bad putters as the stupid adage suggests.

"Let the club head do the work," is just as good advice in putting as in driving. But how much work *is* there in putting—how much pressure does it need to roll a ball four or five yards? Practically none; therefore the tension in our muscular system should be practically nil. The last thing I say to myself before I take my putter back is, "Don't tighten, you old fool."

The next thing I had to work out was which was the primary of those two essentials, strength and direction. And I concluded that strength came first.

Now, before I came to this conclusion, I thought all over and around the subject and studied it in practice, especially in tournament play and in the four-ball exhibition matches which Aubrey and I used to play a great deal ten to eighteen years ago.

I remember holing three successive putts from eight to ten yards in such a match against Jurado and Perrz on the Mar del Plata course. As we walked to the next tee after the third of them went down, Aubrey said to me, "How in the name of fortune do you find the line over these greens?" He might well ask for the greens were terrors! Well, the answer was that I did not try

Putting

deliberately to find the line—I looked for the feel of the *strength* of the shot, and the direction developed out of that feel. That is why I say that strength comes before direction.

How can you learn to develop this sense of direction out of the feeling of strength? Firstly, do not putt at a hole. Just learn how far you can possibly make the ball *roll*. The farther you can make it roll with a given feel of power applied, the better you are stroking the ball. This is an essential study; it is so important that often, when I see people practicing at a hole before a tournament, I feel they would do much better to take at least a few preliminary putts without the preoccupation of the hole at all. The good putter is the one whose ball starts to *roll over as soon as it leaves contact with the club head*.

This rolling over is imparted to the ball by the follow through of the club head, and though it must not be *thought about*, it should be *felt*. The *feel* that we are rolling the ball along is an essential one, and we cannot get it unless we follow through.

The more roll you can give to the ball the farther it will travel in response to a stroke of a given degree of force. In other words, distance depends upon an equation involving both force or power, and roll. There is a maximum to the roll you can produce and consequently a maximum to the distance which you get from a given power. This maximum is known as *dead strength*, and when we can achieve it consistently we

On Learning Golf

can make our putts stop at exactly the distance we desire—exactly hole high. That is why it so often seems, when a really good putter strikes the ball, that it will never be up—yet it creeps on and on and just manages to tumble into the hole.

"Never up, never in," is not the adage of these putters, nor must it be yours. *Dead strength* must be the objective. Putt so that if the hole were *not* there your ball would stop dead on the spot it occupies.

You can do a great deal to develop *dead strength* by constant practice on your carpet. As it develops, a sense of direction will begin to appear, and it is in this sense of direction that you will begin to trust. In fact, you must *feel* direction rather than see it. Of course, what you see with your eyes does help you to find the line, but alone it is not enough.

The sense of feel that guided Hagen when he putted his way round Muirfield in 19 over those fast crinkly greens was something to marvel at. I played over them that day too, and I know! He relied upon perfect stroking to help him find the line, sometimes across as many as three ridges and hollows.

Incidentally, there is one reason not generally appreciated why we Pros take so long looking for the line on the greens in tournament play—it helps us to keep quiet and not to hurry. To see old Ted Ray creeping up to the ball, as he used to do after he had got his line, was a lesson in preparation for a smooth feline stroking of the ball.

Putting

One of the first points to be studied in bringing our putting into line with our other shots is the position from which we play. The first wrong impression we get about putting is that we should be "over the top of the ball." This is often brought about by having too upright a putter and is a great mistake. This being over the ball is the pendulum idea again, with elbows stuck out away from the body.

The good putter feels *inside* the ball, and his elbows, forearms, and left hand are kept very close in—even touching the body. Actually we can stand as near to the ball as the "pendulum down the line of flight" people can, maybe nearer. But with our flatter putter we can keep our hands close in without cocking the toe of the putter up in the air—it can touch the green all along the sole.

Another advantage of not having to feel over the top of the ball is that we can keep well back on our heels, which is an essential to stroking from in-to-out.

About the putter itself. The face of mine is neither too wide nor too short, and its angle is almost 90°, *but not quite* because we need just to see the face. To offset this, the front bottom edge is rounded off so that, if I do come up a little, it is a rounded edge not a sharp one that is presented to the ball. So the bottom edge of the blade is underlapping a concave face from halfway down, a detail which helps toward perfect stroking. Also, I have the top of my shaft, where I grip it, flattened. This I prefer to a square shaft because while

On Learning Golf

it gives the same effect it encourages a lighter touch, and lightness of touch is important.

Now, here is a curious coincidence. I came by this putter almost by accident, in fact it was picked out of a batch as likely "to suit the Boss" by one of my club makers at St. Cloud. Years later curiosity prompted me to measure its lie (the angle between the sole of the blade and the shaft), and I found it to be exactly the same as that of Bobby Jones's famous putter "Calamity Jane."

Now though we must not stand over the ball, we need to be more squat about the knees and hips for the putt than we do for longer shots. Yet above the waist we must feel *up*, because unless we are *up* with our head and shoulders, we cannot feel that we can keep the club head down through the ball.

Next, do not try to take the club head back along the line of flight. Take it back low with the left hand and do not open the blade. If you will study this on a carpet with lines on it, you will find that when you do this the blade goes *inside* in spite of you. This is as it should be; in putting as in driving or playing any other shot, we should not consciously *take* the club inside on the way back; though if we are properly set well back on our heels and keep the putter blade low, that is where it will go.

To *lift* the putter blade back is putting suicide. To keep it low in the follow through is one of the signs of the great artist.

Putting

I feel that I take the putter blade back with the left hand and then roll the ball forward out of my right. The club head and right hand become one in feel. I do not feel that I hit the ball forward but feel that I roll it along from behind. I can feel the ball roll off the face of the putter. In fact when I am putting well, I feel the ball stick for an instant against the face of the putter and then unstick and roll forward as I follow through. With such a feeling, I can be confident that the ball will attain full run *dead strength* as we have called it.

But I warn you that all this will be of no avail if you hold yourself stiffly. To putt well we must be supple and loose. We must not be flabby; we must be conscious of our body being held up by its braces, yet not so braced as to impede movement. All our muscles must be mobilized, *but they must be mobile.* Do not sway to-and-fro, but on the other hand do not get *fixed;* there is a great deal of difference.

Remember that if we are to swing our putter head correctly *every muscle* from head to foot must co-operate. Some of their movements are invisible; some of their changes in tension infinitesimal; yet they are all essential. The putt is just as responsive a movement as is a full shot, and there must be opposition to every movement.

I have told you that I putt as I drive, so the same rules hold. If when you are driving you become a direct hitter, you will begin to pull and slice and exactly

On Learning Golf

the same thing will happen (on a reduced scale of course) if you hit your putts direct.

And to close this chapter I will give you a paradox to think out. No beginner thinks putting difficult; he just goes up to the ball and taps it along to the hole, and as often as not it goes in. It is not until he misses a few as he is bound to do that he forsakes this natural and effective if inelegant style and tries to "learn how"—from then on he becomes an ordinary handicap putter. So here is the paradox: natural golfers are *bad* golfers but natural putters are *good* putters.

CHAPTER XXIII

Interlude for Reminiscence

o

ONE of the perennial joys of golf is the way it fits in with and illuminates the character of the fellow who knows all about it: The Omniscient Golf Maniac.

There are more maniacs in golf than there are in any other sport, and they have more fun too! You see, the golf swing is such an unknown equation to most people that any fellow with the gift of gab and twenty years' experience of pulling and slicing can make it *sound* as though he knows what he is talking about when he expounds it.

There are five or six of these cranks in nearly every club, and when they get together the feathers are apt to fly! The one characteristic of every member of the clan is that he is entirely impervious to every idea and theory except his own.

I remember three of these fellows all round about the (sympathetic) 3 handicap mark having a rabid argument in our shop about that fertile subject, the shut face, and proving—to their own satisfaction anyway—that one or two suggestions that Aubrey and I made were nonsense.

Well then, they took Aubrey out into a four-ball. They gave him one up and he proceeded to beat their

On Learning Golf

best ball 4 and 3. They were so wrapped up in their own game and their own theories that they failed to notice that he had gone round in 64, which was eight under par.

Still, when they came back they continued to tell us how to take the club back and so on. They knew Aubrey had just beaten them, but it never occurred to them that he knew more about golf than they did.

We Pros do know quite a bit about the game. If we seem to differ a lot in our methods, it is because method is not the ultimate aim in golf, and methods (like fashions) are always changing.

One thing that the Pro nearly always has and the maniac nearly always lacks is a balanced psychophysical conception of how to go about the game so as to get par figures for 18 holes in a round for four rounds in succession, or a dozen if necessary.

These cranks spend the greater part of their lives not so much hitting the ball as figuring out *how* to hit it. They will tell you they are realists but actually they are the most visionary idealists in the world to-day! Their world is utterly remote from reality.

There was a time when I used to play a lot with a very wealthy old boy; he was about sixty and had been a crack polo player in his youth. He was 3 handicap and never could take strokes from me, but one Boxing Day (it being the day after Christmas) he beat me.

Well, for a few years after that I did not see him again (yes *years* not days), and I forgot the incident

Interlude for Reminiscence

and nearly forgot him. Then one day when I was out he turned up to ask me to fix a game with him any day I liked.

When the assistant gave me the message he said, "You look surprised!" "Well it is odd," said I. "I haven't seen him for years." My assistant grinned. "That's it," he said. "The story of how he beat you is getting a bit stale, so he wants to freshen it up!" Well, believe it or not, that *was* his idea, so I took care to beat *him* as early as I could, which was on the 13th. So on the way back he consoled himself by telling me again that if he had taken up the game younger he would have won the Championship. Well, maybe he would!

At one time I had under me at St. Cloud three of the finest players ever found together at one club. They were Charles Mignin, a huge driver, a plus 2 player in André Chintron (French champion), and of course my brother Aubrey.

Well, one day an American came up and wanted to play me. It happened that I was engaged, but he was told he could play my assistant. He acquiesced and tumbled into Charles who obliged with a 69. The American thought Charles was very, very good, but he would still like to play me. So he came up again the next day, but his luck was still out, and he accepted a game against André, who turned in a 67. Well, it was almost too good to be true, but next day he missed me once more and took out Aubrey *who went round in 65*.

That fairly shook our friend from the States. "If

On Learning Golf

these are the Assistants," he said "What the hell does the boss go round in—nothing?" Well, he did not see!

One day a very well-known player turned up at St. Cloud and wanted a round with "the boy who did the 61." All he could remember, besides the score, was "Aubrey, St. Cloud."

Aubrey happend to be away so it fell to me to take him round and I turned up a remarkably good round. But I simply could *not* convince him that I was not "Aubrey." So far so good, but then he positively insisted upon me going to dinner with him in Paris. I went full of apprehension which proved justified!

No sooner were we settled in one of the best restaurants in Paris than one of my members caught sight of me and came over, with the typically Parisian greeting, "*Qu'est-ce que tu fais?*—What are you doing here?"

"Oh," said I in French, which I knew my host did not understand, "I am an impostor."

"Why, who are you supposed to be?"

"Aubrey," said I.

"*Nom de Dieu!*" he cried. "*Qui te prend pour Aubrey?*"

I nodded towards my host. The member went over to him, patted him on the shoulder and said in a loud voice in English, "I lift my glass to the finest golfer in France, Aubrey Boomer."

Cheers from all over the room and cries of "Speech! Speech!" Well, of course I had to reply. I did it in French and I can truthfully say that though most of

Interlude for Reminiscence

the laughter that I evoked was at the expense of my blissfully unconscious host—he certainly got more amusement out of the performance than I did!

But to see the Golf Maniac most completely in his element, you want to watch him designing a golf course! We did a lot of that work at one time, both in France and in the Argentine. And it is very difficult to do it well when the club is run by a Green Committee who do not know how much they do not know—and who anyway can never agree among themselves.

I remember on one such occasion we had been tipped not to argue with one old chap who happened to be the Captain of the Club—and felt the responsibility. Well, one day we were fixing the position of the fifth tee and putting it as close as we could get it to a big oak tree for shelter, when up came the Skipper.

He thought we were laying out the fourth green (which we had already placed some thirty yards away) and proceeded to tell us just where and how the bunkers should be arranged. Having finished that he trotted off in high good humor and we did not see him again until the day the course was opened eighteen months later.

For the opening round Aubrey and I played the two local cracks. Among the gallery was our friend the Skipper, and when we reached the fourth green, he sidled up to me.

"I don't remember that tree," he said, pointing to a big beech about twenty yards beyond the green.

On Learning Golf

"Ah, you see," said I "some people are superstitious and won't have an oak tree near a green *or* a beech tree near a tee—so to please them we just changed those two trees round," and I pointed to the oak with the fifth tee beside it.

"Yes! Yes!" he said. "Quite right—and very good of you I'm sure."

As the oak tree was at least three hundred years old and the beech sixty or eighty, the way he accepted that proved (if it proved anything) that *some* people at least have a very high opinion of the capacity of the golf Pro!

But to return to the Golf Bore (as also we so frequently have to!). One world-famous English club numbered one of the greatest among its members. He was no great performer on the course, but in the club room he could (and did) tell exactly how every shot should be played and exactly what and why his partner and opponents had done wrong. *In theory* he was omniscient.

His fellow-members, feeling perhaps that they were too much honored in being the sole recipients of so much golfing wisdom, decided to give it wider circulation. So, to the delight and surprise of the omniscient one there appeared one day on the table in the club reading-room a beautifully bound book titled "All I know about Golf" with the omniscient one's name as author.

Delight and surprise, did I say? Well he was cer-

Interlude for Reminiscence

tainly delighted by the beautifully printed title page (how well his name looked!), by the brief but almost fulsome introduction by an amateur champion, and by the preface by a celebrated golf journalist—the surprise came in the body of the book, where All-he-knew-about-golf was set out on two-hundred-and-forty-six utterly blank pages!

CHAPTER XXIV

Golf Analysis

○

I ASTONISH my pupils when I tell them, as I sometimes do, that for the first twenty years I was teaching golf, I taught it all wrong. They think I am simply decrying my early efforts as a teacher. Actually I tell them this to suggest what an extraordinarily difficult game golf is to analyze and to teach.

You must analyze before you can teach. It is useless just to develop a fine swing yourself and say to your pupil, "Now copy me!" So we must analyze and base our teaching upon what our analysis reveals. But here is a warning—unless your analysis is very deep and close and based upon wide experience, it may mislead you.

Now this is a matter of immediate concern and interest to every advanced golfer whether he wants to be taught or to teach himself. So in this penultimate chapter I will give you a few examples of golf paradoxes which will show you what I mean and point out the sort of traps that golf analysis holds for the unwary. I will start with a question.

Why do you sometimes top your ball?

"That is easy," I can hear you say. "I top my ball when I take my eye off it, because this raises my head

Golf Analysis

which fetches my shoulders up, and *they* pull up my arms—with the natural consequence that I either hit the top of my ball or swing right over it."

Now that or something very like it would be the answer of nine-ninety-nine players out of a thousand. It would have been *my* answer for the first twenty years of my teaching life, but I now know that it is wrong. You do not top the ball because you pull up your body just before impact *but because you drop it*.

You may think that that will take some explaining. It will! Also I can tell you that it took some analyzing to discover.

The first thing to get clear in your mind is the difference between *pulling up* your body and *stretching up through your body*. This latter is essential to one of the most important feels in golf—the feel of *down through the ball*. And it is relevant to note (since it suggests where the ball is contacted) that the higher you want to pitch the ball the more essential is this *down* feeling, a feeling which is the opposite of scooping the club head up.

Now here is another relevant collateral point. When they study film pictures or flickers of great golfers, many people are intrigued and some made quite indignant—to see that some of them are *right up on their toes* during the impact period. And some of the very greatest golfers—Vardon, Bobby Jones, and Miss Joyce Wethered—are the worst "offenders."

Some years ago Mme Lacoste came to me with a

On Learning Golf

photograph of herself driving. She was as far up on her toes as ever Miss Wethered had been. But fortunately by this time I had begun to study and understand the question; so when she asked me what I thought of her picture, I said I saw nothing wrong with it.

"But look," she said, "I am right up on my toes."

"I know you are," said I, "but is that wrong?"

"Every expert I have shown it to says it is."

"Well," says I, "here is one who says it isn't. If you take my advice, you will forget that picture and any idea it has produced in you, and go on playing as you played that shot."

"But it seems all wrong."

"It is *not* all wrong," said I. "Look! your head and shoulders are beautifully *down* and that's all you need to have down. Then see your stretch up through the body—it's marvelous; that is what gives you your wrist snap and makes you such a long hitter for such a little dainty lady."

Now, how does this up-on-the-toes position work in with that point I am always harping on—that the first movement on the return is to bring the left heel solidly and squarely back to the turf?

The return of the left heel to the ground is necessary in order to have an equal balance between the two feet. By the time this balance is achieved, we are nearing the impact—and the stretching up through the

Golf Analysis

body necessary to fling the wrists open reacts as a rising-on-the-toes movement.

You can say that the up-on-the-toes is a reaction to the stretching up through the body or that the effective flinging open of the wrists is a reaction to up-on-the-toes. But whichever way you like to think of it, you will find that the prominent golfer is up-on-the-toes in the region of impact.

Now let me explain the difference between lifting up the shoulders and head and *stretching* up through the body from the feet and legs. You have only to shrug your shoulders to lift them, the stretching is rather more complex. It is an established *feel* in all good golfers that they *stretch down* through their arms as they come into contact with the ball, but you cannot stretch against nothing; so they have to stretch *up* from the feet to set up the necessary resistance in the shoulders. We have to *fix* the top of our swing by giving it something to pull against; otherwise we cannot stretch tautly down from it. We fix the top end by bracing and stretching up to hold our shoulders firmly in place.

If we relax our brace and stretch and let our body sag down ever so little, this top fixing "gives" a little and we no longer keep the feeling of stretching down through the ball. That is where the topped shots come from.

There is a clear difference between *lifting* the shoulders and *holding them up*. If we lift our shoul-

On Learning Golf

ders, we lift our arms out of position, but if we push up from our feet, we may be using equal or greater muscular force simply to hold our shoulder in position against the terrific down-pull of the club head. Consequently, we may even *feel* that we are rising up when actually we are doing no more than resisting in an upward direction the force of the club head which is pulling down. That is why you may find, if you study a whole film with an up-on-the-toes finish, that, in spite of the up-on-the-toes movement, the head and shoulders have not been raised even a fraction of an inch.

If you wish to analyze these movements in yourself by feel, do not try it with your long clubs first. The difference between the feels of lifting the body and of holding the shoulders up through the feet is subtle, so subtle that it is easily lost in the violence of a long shot. You will recognize it much more quickly with a mashie-niblick. The feeling you want is not a gross one, but a feel that we stretch upward against the ground with our legs and feet—gradually and without haste. The push of the ground opposes the pull of the club head.

All golf is opposition. We are in a state of opposing in every phase of our swing, even in the waggle. *The very feel of the club head is only sensed when we are in a state of opposition to it.*

Close students of the game will have noticed that the body sags down as the club reaches the top, so that the player's head may be inches closer to the ball at the

Golf Analysis

apex of the swing; the player is thus opposing and retaining the feel of the club head. At the bottom of the swing the forces and positions will be reversed. The body comes down when the club head is up and goes up as the club head comes down. Opposition again. These up and down movements are not something we do consciously; they are automatic adjustments of balance in opposition.

To return to the upward stretch. Some of you may have been told in a more elaborate phrase to "elongate the left side." This, I think, is a bad doctrine. It does result in some sort of stretch, but an unbalanced one—and one of its most direct results is the plunging right shoulder. We must stretch through the whole center of our equilibrium, right side as well as left, right foot as well as left, right shoulder as well as left.

The plunging right shoulder is fatal because if your right shoulder dips below its correct position relative with the left, you cannot go on through the ball—you become *blocked* just as you get past the ball. The right shoulder must be felt to come square against the back of the ball, neither under nor above it.

This dipping is a fault of the right hip as well as the right shoulder. One is the counterpart of the other. When we see a fellow with his club and hands curled around his left leg at the finish, we know that his right side has buckled on the way down, and so his follow through has been blocked.

Now let us go into this question of the right shoulder

THE SWING

POINTS TO STUDY

Obviously a very young swing, not faultless, but fundamentally good.

1. A wide swing. Left arm straight, left wrist fully broken back. The shoulders are still turned away from the ball while the hips are turned towards it, giving body flail.

2. The left leg has straightened, but the wrists are still broken back.

3. Shoulders now square with the line of flight. Up on the toes, stretching upwards through the body so that the wrists will snap open downwards.

4. Left heel back to the ground. Head still down. Right arm straight . . . elbows still held together.

In the sequence, the hands, and consequently the club head, have come *down yet along*.

FAULTS

In position 2 and 3 the right leg is too stiff.

He is looking at the ball with his right eye instead of "peeping at it with his left eye."

THE SWING 1, 2, 3, 4

GEORGE

(Age 17)

Golf Analysis

more minutely. I want you to become much more conscious of your right shoulder than of your left. When my left heel and leg are going forward I feel that my right shoulder goes back, but I have enough experience to know that what is probably happening is that my right shoulder is stationary in relation to the hips. We feel we are pushing it back when actually we are holding it back—but that is the basic difficulty of analyzing golf feels; we mistake opposition for movement.

Let me again stress here why I prefer the word "oppose" to "resist." Resist suggests something static, oppose is resistance in movement. Also, oppose suggests *direction*. If you *resist* a pull you stand stock still and resist with your weight; if you *oppose* a pull you oppose by a pull in the opposite direction, which is what we are continually doing in golf.

A boy with a catapult is a good illustration of opposition; he pulls in the direction opposite to that he wants his shot to take. He stretches his elastic; we must stretch our bodies—only upwards. And the more you can stretch *up*, the more you can feel *down*, which is what I want you to feel beyond everything.

Now I think that a lot of nearly good players would become really good ones if they learned to manage their hips correctly. I talked just now of becoming blocked just past the ball. This is not due (as it is often assumed to be) to faulty arm work, but to allowing the hips to slide out in the direction of the hole

On Learning Golf

—where they effectively stop any chance of the follow through being carried on and around.

If you will brace your hips in the way I have described, you will feel them *as part of a whole* not as a break in that whole. And it is when we feel the hips and waist as a break that we go wrong. Bending at the waist must be due to suppleness of the waist *not* to disarticulation of the hips. Of course, the hips do articulate during the pivot, but they must do so controlled by the brace; they must be moved, but they must not be allowed to slop around.

The braces and stretches of the golf movement, from feet up through the body and down through arms and hands, combine into one *feel*, the feel that we swing our club wide through the ball and on and around the left side. The correct manipulation of the hips enables this feel to be maintained, but if the hips are disarticulated the whole framework of the feel is broken up.

Well, there we are! Just a few of the considerations which arise when we try to analyze that elementary and fatal fault of lifting up. So I hope you will see how essential an accurate analysis is before we can hope to effect a true correction.

CHAPTER XXV

Inverse Functioning

THERE is a curious evolution in the learning of golf which for want of a better phrase I have called inverse functioning. It arises because we have to teach certain movements *directly* in order that they may later be used *indirectly*.

Consider the pivot. We have to teach you how to pivot by telling you or showing you how it is done and asking you to do it that way. That is, we teach it directly as if it were an end in itself. Yet, no good experienced golfer pivots directly like that—*his pivot is the outcome of his correct conception of the follow through.*

The act of pivoting has two basic functions:

(1) to guide the club head,
(2) to generate power.

We know that we must feel that the club head is brought onto the ball *from in-to-out* and that the peak of the activity of the club head is reached two or three feet *beyond* the ball. So we do not hit *at* the ball *or* down the line of flight—and the experienced golfer has found that the pivot is an essential factor in producing the in-to-out sweep, through the ball that he has found to be correct because effective.

249

On Learning Golf

Now it is really important for you to get this difference in outlook or feeling clearly realized, because until you do, you cannot be anything but a mechanical golfer. So I will put the same thing to you in another way. When you watch a good golfer driving, you may feel that he has a perfect conception of the pivot, but you would probably be much nearer the truth in thinking that he had a perfect conception of the follow through.

If you asked that same golfer *how* he pivoted, he would quite possibly propound some involved and elaborate theory to you when actually he would have been more truthful had he said, "I don't really know how I pivot, but I do know that when I feel like I felt today I can sock that ball *miles!*" In other words, again, his beautiful action has evolved *not* out of the study of how to turn his body but out of a feeling of how to swing past the ball.

So, when I explain to a beginner the mechanical workings of the pivot, I know that I am beginning backwards. But, just as soon as I can, I reverse the pupil's conception. As soon as the pivot is sufficiently well established for the pupil to feel the club head move from *in-to-out,* I switch over from the pivot as a movement to be made to the pivot as a means of encouraging the club head to travel from in-to-out. And soon most of the emphasis can be put on the feeling of in-to-out, because if he retains this feel his pivot cannot have been lost.

Inverse Functioning

I have just told you that the pivot has two functions, to guide the club and to generate power. Some good golf analysts combine the two and compare the body to a lever, and while this means practically nothing to the moderate golfer, it *is* suggestive to the top-notcher. For he may feel his body as a steel bar turning around between his two feet, with all the time the bones of his big toes *opposing* the movements of the club head— the extremes of the swing.

We must never lose sight of the fact that we are all in different stages of evolution as golfers and that a technique *or a conception* may be good in one stage and yet disastrous in another. For those who can reach it, the turning bar analogy may be fruitful; it certainly is true as you can feel for yourself that the leverage in golf comes up and out from the bones of the feet.

You will feel it better (even the greatest expert can feel it better) if you swing *without* a club rather than with one. There is so much more going on when you swing a club that delicate feels are more difficult to detect. There is, of course, *still more going on* when we add a ball—and yet more again when it is zero hour and our name is called out on the tee! Do not forget that I was a scratch golfer years before I hit a decent shot off the first tee at Meyrick Park.

What has this to do with our subject? A great deal. The point of this chapter is that, while you have to learn golf by direct mechanics, you must play it—as soon as you are able—*not* mechanically but through

On Learning Golf

your conception of how it should be played and the *feels* which you have built around this conception. The correct conception is the basis, and that is why I have told you in this book many things that are possibly too advanced for you to make practical use of.

You will probably never come up to the standard which I have set you, but if this book has given you a more correct and comprehensive conception of golf movements, you will get nearer to the highest standards than you would have had you been content with a purely mechanical concept. And, which is perhaps equally important, you are much less likely to recede under pressure.

Even if you do recede a little and if you are unable to play your shots in a tournament as well as I have taught you to play them on the practice ground, remember this: Your opponent is equally anxious to win his match; you will *both* (in consequence) fall back from your normal standard—but, other things being equal, the one of you with the more correct and comprehensive conception of the game will fall back the less.

"But," you may say, endeavoring to pull me back to a point from which I may seem to have wandered, "do you suggest that I must not *think* of pivoting?"

That is exactly what I *do* suggest, *if you are ripe for it*. Your shot and my shot both depend upon the pivot. In the early stages you have to concentrate upon pivoting in order to be able to pivot at all. But I have reached

Inverse Functioning

a stage where I can concentrate upon playing a good shot *via* a good follow through which is quite a different outlook.

Do I neglect my pivot in consequence of this? Oh no! I continue to pivot because I know that if I do not I cannot follow through, and I know the consequences of not following through. *Inverse functioning,* that is all! And I do not even follow through because I know I have to but because I feel that there will be no shot unless I do. In fact I have evolved through to *inverse feel.*

On this matter of inverse feel, I must digress for a few minutes. Long before he plays a shot, the first-class golfer has made up his mind how it should feel. The beginner of course has no such pre-shot feeling—which is why he so frequently makes shots which surprise him!

Now I call this pre-shot feeling and its results, *the set.* My dictionary tells me that to "set" is to "put into condition for use," and that is exactly what the set does for a golfer's mechanism. The average golfer walks up to the tee and addresses the ball—we *set ourselves* before we get to the tee and then, through the feeling which the set has produced, address the ball.

Do not think that this is mere playing with words. It is in hard fact one of the fundamental differences between the good golfer and the great one. It will be obvious that, if the set is the state of the feel that precedes the mechanical movements necessary to play

On Learning Golf

the desired shot, then the feeling of the set and the stance which it induces will differ when we play a chip shot to when we play a full drive. For though the principle underlying every golf shot is the same, the manner of approach to the shot in hand will differ with the lie of the ball and the distance it is desired to propel it.

And note also that *the set is not static*. It is an image of the whole operation—stance and swing—and if this image is correct and is correctly followed out by the mechanism of the body, the shot *must* be one hundred per cent effective. The set is the image of the whole operation from stance to follow through.

As I have said before, the swing is a continuous unbroken movement that cannot be cut into sections for analysis. So I was delighted when one day an ardent pupil of mine remarked, "I can now play with my set in motion." I was delighted (1) because he had presented me with a clever piece of sense phraseology, (2) because he must have truly sensed the golf shot in order to be able to make such a remark, and (3) because here was proof that after many years I had been able to teach what I feel to be the correct approach to the matter.

You have only to watch a great golfer to realize how much of his secret lies in his pre-shot attitude and approach. To see him walk up to the ball and address it is all you need to tell you *this is a golfer*. His quality is demonstrated before his actual stroke, which merely confirms it. His set *is* his game.

Inverse Functioning

The set has two practical purposes, to induce the right movements and to eliminate faulty ones. To take the second first, it is through his set that the good golfer feels his faults before he swings; the bad golfer only knows *his* after he has missed his shot.

It is because the good golfer has to induce the right feeling for that to induce the right movements, that men of the quality of Hagen, Cotton, and lately Locke are often blamed for being slow. Personally I don't play slowly, but I certainly cannot play at all unless I have time to contemplate and rehearse my shots. Of course we can exaggerate this, as I think Locke *does*, but we do need *some* time to get ourselves set or "in a condition for use."

Now, let us come back to the pivot and see how the inverse functioning of this is related to the set. When I go up to address my ball, I do not think of pivoting (as you do); I think of following through. I think of the end, not the means. So if you and I are standing together on the tee, I am mentally playing my shot through to a finish while you are preparing to play yours, through your pivot—and it is quite likely that you will never get as far as the follow through except by luck. You will be lucky if you hit the ball; I will be unlucky if I do not hit a one hundred per cent shot, since my feel is based upon what constitutes a good shot, while yours is based upon what prepares the way for the creation of a good shot—obviously much further back in the golf conception.

On Learning Golf

But the beginner or moderate player must not become discouraged. We attain the ultimate in golf by stages of evolution and it is undesirable to jump a stage —those who do usually come a cropper. If our evolution is gradual, it is all the better for it, for each stage is well founded before the next is added. And concepts are like food—they need to be well masticated and digested before they can be any good to you.

There is another aspect of the concepts by which we play that is worth considering. I will illustrate it by listing four things that the good golfer does that the bad golfer cannot or does not do. The good golfer:

(1) Twists his hips *into* the ball.
(2) Thanks to (1), twists his shoulders into the ball.
(3) Thanks to (2), keeps the feel of his club traveling outwards, and
(4) Takes his divot out straight.

Now this is an interesting little study. You will see that 1, 2, and 3 were all directed towards an effort to swing from *in-to-out*—yet as No. 4 proves he has played down the line of flight with his club head. In short No. 4 is a result which can only be brought about by the setting up of 1, 2, and 3, each of which appears to have a different aim.

Actually all the three factors 1, 2, and 3 are illusionary. No. 3 is the easiest to prove this of. It is *only* when we feel that we are swinging from in-to-out that we do play directly down the line of flight and take our divot out straight.

Inverse Functioning

As to points 1 and 2, I suppose nothing in golf so puzzles the poor player as the way in which the good golfer keeps his right hip and shoulder *inside,* instead of letting them slop out and round. Their puzzlement is due as usual to a wrong conception. The bringing down of the right shoulder inside is *not* a thing that is done directly, a mechanical trick to be learned; it is a *result* of the proper conception of the *timing* of the golf swing.

Except for the initial start back from the ball, the golf swing is a one-after-the-other movement. The feet are one extreme of this movement, the club head is the other; the former move through a very small arc, the latter through a wide one. As a result, the feet finish their movement long before the club head does, if both are moving at the same pace as they should be in the initial stage. The bad golfer, finding that his footwork would be completed long before his arms and club head had even got to the top of their arcs, *waits with his feet* so that he can come down with his feet, shoulders, arms, and club head *all* together. This is why he comes down *outside* and is a bad golfer.

Footwork like everything else in the golf swing must be continuous. It is this continuous, unchecked feel that sets up a *flow* of power. And you can only come *inside* with your hips and shoulders if you keep your feet moving continuously *ahead* of your hips and shoulders. This enables you to twist from inside and behind, behind both in *position* and in *time*.

On Learning Golf

If you ask if the *altogether* descent, with feet and hips and shoulders coming in at the same time, inevitably brings the right hip outside and around, I answer that it does, inevitably.

Today you must come down inside and swing from in-to-out to play championship golf. Why today? Well, it was not always so. Vardon, Taylor, and Duncan seldom tried to get inside any shot. Taylor told me himself that he had never been able to play a shot with intentional pull, and Harry Vardon rarely played a wooden shot to the green dead straight; there was almost always a slight fade or slice to it. All of which was due, of course, to having learned with the old "guttie" ball; the chief difficulty with that ball being to make it rise quickly enough out of indifferent lies. Naturally the slightly *cut* shot gave additional lift.

The last of the out-to-in school was George Duncan. I remember vividly the championship occasion on which he had a spoon shot to play to the last hole at Sandwich to get a four and tie with Hagen. He played for a slight slice which did not quite come off—the ball kept dead straight to where he had aimed, to the left-hand side of the green. So he left himself with a chip shot to play and eventually took five.

I was standing behind him when he played the fatal spoon shot, and I realized then that I had witnessed the end of a great school of golfers.

A NOTE ON THE TYPE

The text of this book is set in Caledonia, a Linotype face designed by W. A. Dwiggins, the man responsible for so much that is good in contemporary book design and typography. Caledonia belongs to the family of printing types called "modern face" by printers—a term used to mark the change in style of type-letters that occurred about 1800. It has all the hard-working feet-on-the-ground qualities of the Scotch Modern face plus the liveliness and grace that is integral in every Dwiggins "product" whether it be a simple catalogue cover or an almost human puppet.

The book was composed, printed, and bound by H. Wolff, New York. Typography by James Hendrickson.